Rick Steves

POCKET

ATHENS

Rick Steves with Gene Openshaw
and Cameron Hewitt

Contents

Introduction

Traveling to Athens is like making a pilgrimage to the cradle of our civilization. Romantics can't help but get goose bumps as they kick around the same pebbles that once stuck in Socrates' sandals, with the floodlit Parthenon forever floating ethereally overhead. You'll walk in the footsteps of the great minds that created democracy, philosophy, theater, and more...even when you're dodging motorcycles on "pedestrianized" streets.

While sprawling and congested, the city has a compact, user-friendly tourist zone, with sights such as the Acropolis Museum and the Ancient Agora an easy walk apart. Many locals speak English, major landmarks are well-signed, and most street signs are in both Greek and English.

To Technopolis &
Gazi District

BENAKI MUSEUM
OF ISLAMIC ART

Ag. Anargiri
Square

Iroon
Square

To Central
Market & National
Archaeological Museum

KERAMIKOS
CEMETERY

ERMOU

PSYRRI

M Thissio

ERMOU

ATHINAS

AIOLOU

ATHINAIDOS

THISSIO

VASILIS

IRAKLIDON

NILEOS

AKAMANTOS

TEMPLE
OF
HEPHAISTOS

MAIN AGORA
ENTRANCE

Monastiraki
Square

Monastiraki M

CHURCH OF
KAPNIKAREA

MONASTIRAKI

Cathedral

ANCIENT
AGORA

LIBRARY
OF
HADRIAN

PANDROSSOU

Agora
Square

MUSEUM OF
GREEK
FOLK ART
(2017)

ROMAN
FORUM

APOSTOLOU PAVLOU

Mars
Hill

Pnyx
Hill

PROPYLAEA

ERECHTHEION

ACROPOLIS
ENTRANCE

ANAFIOTIKA

ACROPOLIS

PARTHENON

Nymfon
Hill

ODEON OF
HERODES ATTICUS

DIONYSIOU

AREOPAGITOU

THEATER OF
DIONYSUS

DORA STRATOU
THEATER

Filopappos
Hill

FILOPAPPOS
MONUMENT

MAKRIGIANNI

ACROPOLIS
MUSEUM

MAKRIGIANNI

M

Map Legend

🏞	Viewpoint		Area of Ancient Ruins		Park
♦	Entrance	Ⓣ	Taxi Stand	🅿	Parking
WC	Restroom	Ⓜ Ⓜ Ⓜ	Metro Stop	👥	Tourist Info
🏛	Church	Ⓑ	Bus Stop	■	Statue/Point of Interest

Klafthmonos Square
MUSEUM OF THE CITY OF ATHENS
To Lykavittos Hill
300 Meters
300 Yards
KOLONAKI
STADIOU
PANEPISTIMIOU/ELEFTHERIOU VENIZELOU
KOLOKOTRONI
SYNTAGMA
N
BENAKI MUSEUM OF GREEK HISTORY & CULTURE
MUSEUM OF CYCLADIC ART
To M Evangelismos
PERIKLEOUS
VASILISSIS
NATIONAL WAR MUS.
ERMOU
Syntagma Square
SOFIAS
BYZANTINE & CHRISTIAN MUSEUM
CATHEDRAL (MITROPOLIS)
POST
PARLIAMENT
M Syntagma
To Airport
Bus #X95 to Airport B
PLAKA
VASILISSIS AMALIAS
NATIONAL GARDEN
ADRIANOU
Filomousou Square
ZAPPEION
VASILEOS KONSTANTINOU
ARCH OF HADRIAN
VASILISSIS OLGAS
PANGRATI
Akropoli
TEMPLE OF OLYMPIAN ZEUS
Stadium Square
ATHANASIOU DIAKOU
ARDITTOU
PANATHENAIC STADIUM

) (Tunnel	—— Metro Line
Pedestrian Zone	IIIIIIIII Stairs
------ Railway	..... Walk/Tour Route
.... Ferry/Boat Route	------ Trail

Use this legend to help you navigate the maps in this book.

About This Book

The core of the book is five self-guided tours that zero in on Athens' greatest sights. My Athens City Walk leads you on a three-part stroll through the engaging and refreshingly small city center. My Acropolis and Ancient Agora tours take you back in time to the bustling religious and commercial centers of ancient Greece. And the Acropolis Museum and National Archaeological Museum provide up-close views of artifacts and treasures unearthed from Greece's great ancient sites.

The rest of the book is a traveler's tool kit. You'll find plenty more about Athens' attractions, from shopping to nightlife to less touristy sights. And there are helpful hints on saving money, avoiding crowds, getting around on public transportation, enjoying a great meal, and more.

Key to This Book

Sights are rated:

▲▲▲ **Don't miss**
▲▲ **Try hard to see**
▲ **Worthwhile if you can make it**
No rating **Worth knowing about**

Tourist information offices are abbreviated as **TI**, and bathrooms are **WCs**.

Like Europe, this book uses the **24-hour clock**. It's the same through 12:00 noon, then keep going: 13:00 (1:00 p.m.), 14:00 (2:00 p.m.), and so on.

For **opening times**, if a sight is listed as "May-Oct daily 9:00-16:00," it should be open from 9 a.m. until 4 p.m. from the first day of May until the last day of October (but expect exceptions).

For **updates** to this book, visit www.ricksteves.com/update. For a valuable list of reports and experiences—good and bad—from fellow travelers, check www.ricksteves.com/feedback.

Athens Neighborhoods

NATIONAL ARCHAEOLOGICAL MUSEUM

OMONIA SQUARE

OMONIA

EXARCHIA

NAT'L LIBRARY

LYKAVITTOS HILL

ATHINAS

PANEPISTIMIOU/ ELEFTHERIOU VENIZELOU

KOLONAKI

To Gazi

PSYRRI

SYNTAGMA

VASILISSIS SOFIAS

ERMOU

MONASTIRAKI

THISSIO

AGORA

SYNTAGMA SQUARE

PARLIAMENT

ADRIANOU

PLAKA

National Garden

APOSTOLOU PAVLOU

ACROPOLIS

DIONYSIOU AREOPAGITOU

VASILISSIS AMALIAS

FILOPAPPOS HILL

ACROPOLIS MUSEUM

TEMPLE OF OLYMPIAN ZEUS

MAKRIGIANNI

KOUKAKI

SYNGROU

To Piraeus & Cruise Port

Not to Scale

DCH

Introduction

Athens by Neighborhood

Ninety-five percent of Athens is noisy, polluted modern sprawl, jammed with characterless concrete suburbs—poorly planned and hastily erected to house the area's rapidly expanding population. But most visitors never see that part of Athens. Almost everything of importance to tourists is within a few blocks of the Acropolis.

A good map is a necessity for enjoying Athens on foot. The fine map the tourist info office (TI) gives out works great. You'll concentrate on the following districts:

The Plaka (PLAH-kah, Πλάκα in Greek): This neighborhood at the foot of the Acropolis is the core of the tourist's Athens. One of the only

Athens at a Glance

▲▲▲**Acropolis** The most important ancient site in the Western world, where Athenians built their architectural masterpiece—the Parthenon. **Hours:** Daily May-Sept 8:00-20:00, April and Oct 8:00-19:00, Nov-March 8:00-15:00. See page 41.

▲▲▲**Acropolis Museum** Glassy modern temple for ancient art. **Hours:** Mon 8:00-16:00, Tue-Sun 8:00-20:00, Fri until 22:00. See page 87.

▲▲▲**Ancient Agora** Social and commercial center of ancient Athens, with a well-preserved temple and intimate museum. **Hours:** Same hours as the Acropolis. See page 69.

▲▲▲**National Archaeological Museum** World's best collection of ancient Greek art. **Hours:** April-Oct daily 8:00-20:00; Nov-March Mon 12:00-17:00, Tue-Sun 8:00-15:00. See page 99.

▲▲**"Acropolis Loop"** Traffic-free pedestrian walkways ringing the Acropolis with vendors, cafés, and special events. See page 122.

▲▲**Temple of Olympian Zeus** Remains of the largest temple in ancient Greece. **Hours:** Same hours as the Acropolis. See page 128.

▲▲**Benaki Museum of Greek History and Culture** Exquisite collection of artifacts from the ancient, Byzantine, Ottoman, and modern eras. **Hours:** Wed and Fri 9:00-17:00, Thu and Sat 9:00-24:00, Sun 9:00-15:00, closed Mon-Tue. See page 131.

parts of town that's atmospheric and Old World-feeling, it's also the most crassly touristic (souvenir shops and tacky tavernas).

Monastiraki (mah-nah-stee-RAH-kee, Μοναστηρακι): This area ("Little Monastery") borders the Plaka to the northwest, surrounding the square of the same name. It has a handy Metro stop (where line 1/green meets line 3/blue), seedy flea market, and souvlaki stands.

Psyrri (psee-REE, Ψυρή): Formerly a dumpy ghetto just north of Monastiraki, Psyrri is now a cutting-edge nightlife and dining district—and one of central Athens' most appealing areas to explore after dark.

Syntagma (SEEN-dag-mah, Συνταγμα): Centered on Athens' main square, Syntagma ("Constitution") Square, this urban-feeling zone melts into the Plaka to the south and is bounded to the east by the Parliament

▲▲**Museum of Cycladic Art** World's largest compilation of Cycladic art, from 4,000 years ago. **Hours:** Mon and Wed-Sat 10:00-17:00, Thu until 20:00, Sun 11:00-17:00, closed Tue. See page 132.

▲▲**Byzantine and Christian Museum** Fascinating look at the Byzantines, who put their own stamp on a flourishing culture. **Hours:** April-Oct daily 8:00-20:00; Nov-March Tue-Sun 9:00-16:00, closed Mon. See page 133.

▲**Mars Hill** Historic spot—with a classic view of the Acropolis—where the Apostle Paul preached to the Athenians. **Hours:** Always open. See page 122.

▲**Syntagma Square** Athens' most famous public space, with a popular changing-of-the-guard ceremony. **Hours:** Guards change five minutes before the top of each hour, full ceremony with marching band on Sun at 11:00. See page 126.

▲**Panathenaic (a.k.a. "Olympic") Stadium** Gleaming marble stadium restored to its second-century A.D. condition. **Hours:** Daily March-Oct 8:00-19:00, Nov-Feb 8:00-17:00. See page 129.

Opening hours for sights in Greece can change without notice, so be sure to confirm hours locally.

building and the National Garden. While the Plaka is dominated by tourist shops, Syntagma is where local urbanites do their shopping.

Thissio (thee-SEE-oh, Θησείο): West of the Ancient Agora, Thissio is an upscale, local-feeling residential neighborhood with piles of outdoor cafés and restaurants. It's easily accessible thanks to the handy pedestrian walkway around the Acropolis.

Makrigianni (mah-kree-YAH-nee, Μακρυγιάννη) and **Koukaki** (koo-KAH-kee, Κουκάκι): Tucked just behind (south of) the Acropolis, these overlapping urban neighborhoods have a lived-in charm and make a good home base.

Kolonaki (koh-loh-NAH-kee, Κολωνάκι): Just north and east of the Parliament/Syntagma Square area, this upscale diplomatic quarter, with several good museums and a yuppie dining zone, huddles under the tall, pointy Lykavittos Hill.

Major Streets: The Acropolis is ringed by a broad traffic-free walkway, named **Dionysiou Areopagitou** (Διονυσίου Αρεοπαγίτου) to the south and **Apostolou Pavlou** (Αποστόλου Παύλου) to the west; for simplicity, I call these the **"Acropolis Loop."** Touristy **Adrianou** street (Αδριανού) curves through the Plaka a few blocks away from the Acropolis' base. Partly pedestrianized **Ermou** street (Ερμού) runs west from Syntagma Square, defining the Plaka, Monastiraki, and Thissio to the south, and Psyrri to the north. Where Ermou meets Monastiraki, **Athinas** street (Αθηνάς) heads north to Omonia Square.

Planning Your Time

The Acropolis/Ancient Agora, the Acropolis Museum, and the National Archaeological Museum deserve a half-day each. Two days' total is plenty of time for the casual tourist to see the city's main attractions.

Day 1: In the morning, follow my Athens City Walk. Grab a souvlaki lunch near Monastiraki, and spend midday in the markets (shopping in the Plaka, browsing in the Central Market, and wandering through the flea market—best on Sun). After lunch, as the crowds (and heat) subside, visit the ancient biggies: First tour the Ancient Agora, then hike up to the Acropolis (carefully confirming how late it's open). Be the last person off the Acropolis. Stroll down the Dionysiou Areopagitou pedestrian boulevard, then promenade to dinner—in Thissio, Monastiraki, Psyrri, or the Plaka.

Day 2: Spend the morning visiting the Acropolis Museum and exploring the Plaka. After lunch, head to the National Archaeological Museum.

Day 3 and Beyond: Head out to Kolonaki to take in some of Athens' lesser sights—the Benaki Museum of Greek History and Culture, Museum

Daily Reminder

Sunday: Most sights are open, but the Central Market is closed. The Monastiraki flea market is best to visit today. An elaborate changing of the guard—including a marching band—takes place at 11:00 in front of the Parliament building. State-run sights and museums, including the Acropolis, are free on the first Sunday of the month during off-season (Nov-March).

Monday: Many museums and galleries are closed, including the Benaki Museum of Greek History and Culture, Benaki Museum of Islamic Art, Byzantine and Christian Museum, and National War Museum.

Tuesday: These sights are closed today: the Museum of Cycladic Art, Benaki Museum of Islamic Art, and Benaki Museum of Greek History and Culture.

Wednesday: The Benaki Museum of Islamic Art is closed.

Thursday: All major sights are open.

Friday: All major sights are open.

Saturday: All major sights are open.

Evening Sightseeing: Many sights are open late in summer, often until 20:00. Some sights are open until 20:00 year-round, including the Acropolis Museum (Tue-Sun; Fri until 22:00) and Museum of Cycladic Art (Thu only). The Benaki Museum of Greek History and Culture is open Thursday and Saturday until 24:00.

of Cycladic Art, and Byzantine and Christian Museum. Or consider ditching Athens for a long but satisfying side-trip to Delphi, a sweet getaway to the isle of Hydra, or a quick dip into the Peloponnese peninsula, with the charming port town of Nafplio and the famous ancient sites of Epidavros and Mycenae. Even better, spend the night.

These are busy day-plans, so be sure to schedule in slack time for picnics, laundry, people-watching, leisurely dinners, shopping, and recharging your touristic batteries. Slow down and be open to unexpected experiences and the hospitality of the Greek people.

Trip Tips: The Acropolis combo-ticket covers entry to Athens' major ancient sites, including the Acropolis and Ancient Agora (see page 123 for more info).

Don't put off visiting a must-see sight. The hours for sights in Greece are often in flux, and with government spending cuts, some sights have reduced hours. I've listed the posted hours, but check locally for the most up-to-date information.

🎧 Download my free Athens audio tours—covering the Acropolis, Ancient Agora, National Archaeological Museum, and Athens City Walk—onto your mobile device and bring them along. For more on these, plus other sightseeing tips, see page 167.

A word about travel safety: Because of Greece's "economic meltdown," there have been demonstrations and occasional riots. But most rallies involve zero violence. When violence has broken out, it's all been strictly between police and protesters, not bystanders...and certainly not tourists out for a stroll.

I hope you have a great trip! Traveling like a temporary local and taking advantage of the information here, you'll enjoy the absolute most out of every mile, minute, and euro. I'm happy that you'll be visiting places I know and love, and meeting some of my favorite Greek people.

Happy travels! *Kalo taxidi!*

Athens City Walk

From Syntagma Square to Monastiraki Square

This walk takes you through the striking contrasts of the city center—from chaotic, traffic-clogged urban zones, to sleepy streets packed with bearded priests shopping for a new robe or chalice, to peaceful back lanes barely wide enough for a donkey that twist their way up toward the Acropolis. The walk begins at Syntagma Square, meanders through the fascinating old Plaka district, and finishes at lively Monastiraki Square (near the Ancient Agora, markets, good restaurants, and a handy Metro stop). This sightseeing spine will help you get a once-over-lightly look at Athens, which you can use as a springboard for diving into the city's various colorful sights and neighborhoods.

ORIENTATION

Churches: Athens' churches keep irregular hours, but they're generally open daily 8:30-13:30 & 17:00-19:30. If you want to buy candles at churches (as the locals do), be sure to have a few small coins.

Cathedral: Generally open daily 8:00-13:00 & 16:30-19:00, no afternoon closure in summer.

Temple of Olympian Zeus: €6, covered by Acropolis combo-ticket, daily May-Sept 8:00-20:00, April and Oct 8:00-19:00, Nov-March 8:00-15:00, Vasilissis Olgas 1, Metro: Akropoli, tel. 210-922-6330, www.culture.gr.

Roman Forum: €6, covered by Acropolis combo-ticket, daily 8:00-15:00, possibly open later in summer, corner of Pelopida and Aiolou streets, Metro: Monastiraki, tel. 210-324-5220, www.culture.gr.

Library of Hadrian: €4, covered by Acropolis combo-ticket, daily 8:00-15:00, possibly open later in summer, across from Agora Square, Metro: Monastiraki.

When to Go: Do this walk early in your visit, as it can help you get your bearings in this potentially confusing city. Morning is best, since many churches close for an afternoon break and other sights—such as the Acropolis—are too crowded to enjoy.

Dress Code: Wearing shorts inside churches is frowned upon, though usually tolerated.

Getting There: The walk begins at Syntagma Square, just northeast of the Plaka tourist zone. It's a short walk from my recommended Plaka hotels; if you're staying away from the city center, get here by Metro (stop: Syntagma).

Audio Tour: ∩ Download my free Athens City Walk audio tour.

Length of This Walk: Allow plenty of time. This three-part walk takes two hours without stops or detours. But if you explore and dip into sights here and there—pausing to ponder a dimly lit Orthodox church, or doing some window (or actual) shopping—it can enjoyably eat up a half-day or more. If you find this walk too long, it's easy to break up—stop after Part 2 and return for Part 3 at a different time or on another day.

Starring: Athens' top squares, churches, and Roman ruins, connected by bustling urban streets that are alternately choked with cars and mopeds, or thronged by pedestrians, vendors...and fellow tourists.

THE WALK BEGINS

This lengthy walk is thematically divided into three parts: The first part focuses on modern Athens, centered on Syntagma Square and the Ermou shopping street. The second part focuses on Athens' Greek Orthodox faith, with visits to three different but equally interesting churches. And the third part is a wander through the charming old core of Athens, including the touristy Plaka and the mellow Greek-village-on-a-hillside of Anafiotika.

PART 1: MODERN ATHENS

This part of our walk lets you feel the pulse of a European capital.

▸ *Start at Syntagma Square. From the leafy park at the center of the square, climb to the top of the stairs (in the middle of the square) and stand across the street from the big, Neoclassical Greek Parliament building.*

❶ Syntagma Square (Plateia Syntagmatos)

As you look at posh hotels and major banks, you are standing atop the city's central Metro stop, surrounded by buses, cars, and taxis. Facing the Parliament building (east), get oriented to the square named for Greece's constitution (*syntagma;* SEEN-dag-mah). From this point, sightseeing options spin off through the city like spokes on a wheel.

Fronting the square on the left (north) side are high-end hotels, including the opulent Hotel Grande Bretagne (with its swanky rooftop garden restaurant).

Directly to the left of the Parliament building is the head of Vasilissis Sofias avenue, lined with embassies and museums, including the Benaki Museum of Greek History and Culture, Museum of Cycladic Art, Byzantine and Christian Museum, and National War Museum. This boulevard leads to the ritzy Kolonaki quarter, with its funicular up to the top of Lykavittos Hill. Extending to the right of the Parliament building is the National Garden, Athens' "Central Park." Here you'll find the Zappeion mansion-turned-conference-hall (with a fine summer outdoor cinema nearby) and, beyond the greenery, the evocative, ancient Panathenaic Stadium.

On your right (south) is one of Athens' prime transit hubs, with stops

Athens City Walk

SYNTAGMA

HOTEL GRANDE
BRETAGNE

To
Kolonaki &
Lykavittos
Hill

PERIKLEOUS

KARA. SERV.

Bus #X80
to / from Piraeus

VAS. SOFIAS

ERMOU

VAS. GEORGIOU

WALK
BEGINS

TOMB OF
THE UNKNOWN
SOLDIER

CATHEDRAL
(MITROPOLIS)

PETRAKI

Syntagma
Square

PARLIAMENT

MITROPOLEOS

POST

OTHONOS

THEODOR-
OPOULOS
SHOP

APOLLONOS

Bus #040
to Piraeus

STOAS

AG.
FILOTHEIS

NIKODIMOU

JEWISH
MUSEUM

IPERIDOU

PLAKA

SOTIROS

KIDATHINEON

Filomousou
Square

DEDALOU

AG.
AIKATERINI

THOLOU

SHELLY

GOURA

PITTAKOU

LYSIKRATOUS

LYSICRATES
MONUMENT

ARCH OF
HADRIAN

Bus #X80
from Piraeus

Bus #X80
to Piraeus

Akropoli

TEMPLE OF
OLYMPIAN ZEUS

1. Syntagma Square
2. Tomb of the Unknown
   Soldier & Evzone Guards
3. Parliament
4. Hotel Grande Bretagne
5. Ermou Street
6. Church of Kapnikarea
7. Cathedral & Square
8. Church of Agios Eleftherios
9. Agia Filotheis Street
10. Church of Agia Filotheis
11. Adrianou Street
12. Arch of Hadrian &
    Temple of Olympian Zeus
13. Lysicrates Monument &
    Square
14. View of Lykavittos Hill
15. Anafiotika
16. Roman Forum &
    Tower of the Winds
17. Agora Square
18. Library of Hadrian
19. Monastiraki Square
20. "Souvlaki Row"
21. Former Mosque &
    Ceramics Museum
22. Ancient Agora
23. Flea Market
24. Monastiraki Metro Stn.

Syntagma Square—center of modern Athens.

National Garden—Athens' Central Park.

for bus #X95 to the airport, and the Athens Coastal Tram. Beneath your feet is the Syntagma Metro station, the city's busiest.

Behind you, at the west end of the square, stretches the traffic-free shopping street called Ermou, which heads to the Plaka neighborhood and Monastiraki Square. (We'll be heading that way soon.) Nearby is the terminus for one of Athens' two tourist trains (see page 172).

Plane trees, cypress, and laurel make Syntagma a breezy and restful spot. Breathe deeply and ponder the fact that until 1990, Athens was the most polluted city in Europe. People advertising facial creams would put a mannequin outside on the street for three hours and film it turning black. The message: You need our cream.

But over the last two decades, "green" policies have systematically cleaned up the air. Traffic, though still pretty extreme, is limited: Even- and odd-numbered license plates are prohibited in the center on alternate days (though downtown residents are exempt). Check the license plates of passing cars (not taxis or motorcycles): The majority end with either an even or an odd number, depending on the day of the week. While car traffic is down, motorcycle usage is up (since bikes are exempt). Central-heating fuel is more expensive and much cleaner these days (as required by European Union regulations), more of the city center is pedestrianized, and the city's public transport is top-notch.

▶ *Using the crosswalk (one on either side of Syntagma Square), cross the busy street. Directly in front of the Parliament you'll see the...*

❷ Tomb of the Unknown Soldier and the Evzone Guards
Standing amid pigeons and tourists in front of the imposing Parliament building, overlooking Syntagma Square, you're at the center of Athens'

modern history. Above the simple marble-slab tomb—marked only with a cross—is a carved image of the Unknown Soldier, a heavily armed dying Greek, inspired by the statue of a dying nude from the ancient Aphaia temple on the island of Aigina, very close to Athens. Etched into the stone on each side of the tomb are the names of great battles in Greek military history from 1821 forward (practice your Greek alphabet by trying to read them: Cyprus, Korea, Rimini, Crete, and so on).

The tomb is guarded by the much-photographed evzone, an elite infantry unit of the Greek army. The guard changes five minutes before the top of each hour, with a less elaborate crossing of the guard at :25 after. They march with a slow-motion, high-stepping march to their new positions, then stand ramrod straight, where you can pose alongside them. A full changing-of-the-guard ceremony, complete with marching band, takes place on Sundays at 11:00 (arrive a bit early).

These colorful characters are clad in traditional pleated kilts *(fustanella),* white britches, and pom-pom shoes. (The outfits may look a little goofy to a non-Greek, but their mothers and girlfriends are very proud.) The uniforms, worn everywhere in Greece, were made famous by the Klephts, ragtag bands of mountain guerrilla fighters. After nearly four centuries under the thumb of the Ottoman Empire (from today's Turkey, starting in 1453), the Greeks rose up. The Greek War of Independence (1821-1829) pitted the powerful Ottoman army against the lowly but wily Klephts. The soldiers' skirts have 400 pleats...one for each year of Ottoman occupation (and don't you forget it). Although considered heroes today for their courage, outrageous guerrilla tactics, and contribution to the Liberation Army in the 19th century, the Klephts were once regarded as warlike bandits (their name shares a root with the English word "kleptomania").

Evzone guards at the tomb.

Their colorful outfits draw a crowd.

As the Klephts and other Greeks fought for their independence, a number of farsighted Europeans (including the English poet Lord Byron)—inspired by the French Revolution and their own love of ancient Greek culture—came to their aid. In 1829, the rebels finally succeeded in driving their Ottoman rulers out of central Greece, and there was a movement to establish a modern democracy. However, the Greeks were unprepared to rule themselves, and so, after the Ottomans came...Otto.

▶ *For the rest of the story, take a step back for a view of the...*

❸ Parliament

The origins of this "palace of democracy" couldn't have been less democratic. The first independent Greek government, which had its capital in Nafplio, was too weak to be viable. As was standard operating procedure at that time, the great European powers forced Greece to accept a king from established European royalty.

In 1832, Prince Otto of Bavaria became King Otto of Greece. A decade later, after the capital shifted to Athens, this royal palace was built to house King Otto and his wife, Queen Amalia. The atmosphere was tense. After fighting so fiercely for its independence from the Ottomans, the Greeks now chafed under royal rule from a dictatorial Bavarian monarch. The palace's over-the-top luxury only angered impoverished locals.

On September 3, 1843, angry rioters gathered in the square to protest, demanding a democratic constitution. King Otto stepped onto the balcony of this building, quieted the mob, and gave them what they wanted. The square was dubbed Syntagma (Constitution), and modern Athens was born. The former royal palace has been the home of the Greek parliament since 1935. Today this is where 300 Greek parliamentarians (elected

Parliament overlooking Syntagma Square.

Neoclassical Hotel Grande Bretagne.

to four-year terms) tend to the business of the state—or, as more cynical locals would say, become corrupt and busily get themselves set up for their cushy, post-political lives.

▶ *Cross back to the heart of Syntagma Square, and focus on the grand building fronting its north side.*

❹ Hotel Grande Bretagne and Neoclassical Syntagma

Imagine the original Syntagma Square (which was on the outskirts of town in the early 19th century): a big front yard for the new royal palace, with the country's influential families building mansions around it. Surviving examples of 19th-century architecture—as well as more modern buildings renovated in a neo-Neoclassical style so they'd fit in—include Hotel Grande Bretagne, the adjacent Hotel King George Palace, the Zappeion in the National Garden (not visible from here), and the stately architecture lining Vasilissis Sofias avenue behind the palace (now embassies and museums).

Many of these grand buildings date from Athens' Otto-driven Neoclassical makeover. Eager to create a worthy capital for Greece, Otto imported teams of Bavarian architects to draft a plan of broad avenues and grand buildings in what they imagined to be the classical style. This "Neoclassical" look is symmetrical and geometrical, with pastel-colored buildings highlighted in white trim. The windows are rectangular, flanked by white Greek half-columns (pilasters), fronted by balconies, and topped with cornices. Many of the buildings are also framed at the top with cornices. As you continue on this walk, notice not only the many Neoclassical buildings, but also the more modern buildings that try to match the same geometric lines.

Syntagma Square is also worth a footnote in American Cold War history. In December 1944, Greek communists demonstrated here, inducing the US to come to the aid of the Greek government. This became the basis (in 1947) for the Truman Doctrine, which pledged US aid to countries fighting communism and helped shape American foreign policy for the next 50 years.

▶ *Head down to the bottom of Syntagma (directly across from the Parliament). Stroll down the traffic-free street near the McDonald's.*

❺ Ermou Street

The pedestrian mall called Ermou (AIR-moo) leads from Syntagma down through the Plaka to Monastiraki, then continues westward to the ancient

Keramikos Cemetery and the Gazi district. Not long ago, this street epitomized all that was terrible about Athens: lousy building codes, tacky neon signs, double-parked trucks, and noisy traffic. When Ermou was first pedestrianized in 2000, merchants were upset. Now they love the ambience created as countless locals stroll through what has become a people-friendly shopping zone.

This has traditionally been the street of women's shops. However, these days Ermou is dominated by high-class international chain stores, which appeal to young Athenians but turn off older natives, who lament the lack of local flavor. For authentic, hole-in-the-wall shopping, many Athenians prefer the streets just to the north, such as Perikleous, Lekka, and Kolokotroni (for shopping tips, see the Practicalities chapter).

Even so, this people-crammed boulevard is a pleasant place for a wander. Do just that, proceeding gradually downhill and straight ahead for seven blocks. As you window-shop, notice that some of Ermou's department stores are housed in impressive Neoclassical mansions. Talented street performers provide an entertaining soundtrack. All of Athens walks along here: businesspeople, teenage girls with iPhones, Orthodox priests, activists gathering signatures, illegal vendors who sweep up their wares and scurry when they see police, and, of course, tourists. Keep an eye out for vendors selling various snacks—including pretzel-like sesame rings called *koulouri* and slices of fresh coconut.

After six short blocks, on the right (at the intersection with Evangelistrias/Ευαγγελιστριασ), look for the little **book wagon** selling cheap lit. You'll likely see colorful, old-fashioned alphabet books (labeled ΑΛΦΑΒΗΤΑΡΙΟ, *Alphabetario*), which have been reprinted for nostalgic older Greeks. Remember that the English word "alphabet" comes from the first two Greek letters (alpha, beta).

PART 2: THE GREEK ORTHODOX CHURCH

In the fourth century A.D., the Roman Empire split in half, dividing Eastern Europe and the Balkan Peninsula down the middle. Seven centuries later, with the Great Schism, the Christian faith diverged along similar lines, into two separate branches: Roman Catholicism in the west (based in Rome) and Eastern or Byzantine Orthodoxy in the east (based in Constantinople—today's Istanbul). Rather than having one centralized headquarters (such as the Vatican for Catholicism), the Eastern Orthodox Church is divided into about a dozen regional branches (such as the Russian Orthodox Church and the Greek Orthodox Church), each remaining administratively independent. This part of our walk introduces you to the Orthodox faith of Greece, including stops at three churches.

▶ *Stranded in the middle of both Ermou street and the commercial bustle of the 21st century is a little medieval church.*

❻ Church of Kapnikarea

After the ancient Golden Age, but before Otto and the Ottomans, Athens was part of the Byzantine Empire (A.D. 323-1453). In the 11th and 12th centuries, Athens boomed, and several Eastern Orthodox churches like this one were constructed.

The Church of Kapnikarea is a classic 11th-century Byzantine church. Notice that it's square and topped with a central dome. Telltale signs of a Byzantine church include tall arches over the windows, stones surrounded by a frame of brick and mortar, and a domed cupola with a cross on top. The large white blocks are scavenged from other, earlier monuments (also typical of Byzantine churches from this era). Over the door is a mosaic

Church of Kapnikarea—"icon"-ic Orthodox in the middle of trendy Ermou street.

Kapnikarea, with a traditional Byzantine-style mosaic over the door.

of glass and gold leaf, which, though modern, is made in the traditional Byzantine style.

Step inside if the church is open. (If it's closed, don't fret—we'll be visiting a couple of similar churches later.) Notice the Greek-cross floor plan and the early 20th-century, modern-yet-still-medieval art. It's decorated with standing candelabras, hanging lamps, tall arches, a wooden pulpit, and a few chairs. If you wish, you can do as the Greeks do and follow the standard candle-buying, icon-kissing ritual (see sidebar on page 26). The icon displayed closest to the door gets changed with the church calendar. You may notice lipstick smudges on the protective glass and a candle-recycling box behind the candelabra.

Look up into the central dome, lit with windows, which symbolizes heaven. Looking back down is the face of Jesus, the omnipotent *Pantocrator* God blessing us on Earth. He holds a Bible in one hand and blesses us with the other. On the walls are iconic murals of saints. Notice the focus on the eyes, which are considered a mirror of the soul and a symbol of its purity.

▶ *When you leave the church, turn south toward the Acropolis and proceed downhill on Kapnikareas street. Up ahead, catch a glimpse of the*

Acropolis. Go two blocks to the traffic-free Pandrossou shopping street. Turn left and walk up the pedestrian street to the cathedral.

❼ Cathedral (Mitropolis) and Cathedral Square (Plateia Mitropoleos)

Built from 1842 to 1862, this "metropolitan church" (as the Greek Orthodox call their cathedrals) is the most important in Athens, which makes it the head church of the Greek Orthodox faith. Unfortunately, it's unremarkable and oddly ramshackle inside and out...and has been decorated with scaffolding since the earthquake of 1999.

If it's open, head inside. Looking up, you'll notice balconies. Traditionally, women worshipped apart from men in the balconies upstairs. Women got the vote in Greece in 1952, and since about that time, they've been able to worship in the prime, ground-floor real estate alongside the men.

When you're back outside on the square, notice the statue facing the cathedral. This was erected by Athens' Jewish community as thanks to **Archbishop Damaskinos** (1891-1949), the rare Christian leader who stood up to the Nazis during the occupation of Greece. At great personal risk, Damaskinos formally spoke out against the Nazi occupiers on behalf of the Greek Jews he saw being deported to concentration camps. When a Nazi commander threatened to put Damaskinos before a firing squad, the archbishop defiantly countered that he should be hanged instead, in good Orthodox tradition. After the occupation, Damaskinos served as regent and then prime minister of Greece until the king returned from exile.

Here Damaskinos is depicted wearing the distinctive hat of an archbishop (a kind of fez with cloth hanging down the sides). He carries a staff and blesses with his right hand, making a traditional Orthodox sign of the

Orthodox cathedral, with scaffolding.

Archbishop making the sign of Jesus.

Rituals of the Eastern Orthodox Church

While the doctrine of Catholic and Orthodox churches remains very similar, many of the rituals are different. As you enter any Greek Orthodox church, you can join in the standard routine: Drop a coin in the wooden box, pick up a candle, say a prayer, light the candle, and place it in the candelabra. Make the sign of the cross and kiss the icon.

Worshippers stand through the service as a sign of respect (though some older parishioners sit on the seats along the walls). Traditionally, women stand on the left side, men on the right (but are an equal distance from the altar—to represent that all are equal before God). Orthodox services generally involve chanting (a dialogue that goes back and forth between the priest and the congregation), and the church is filled with the evocative aroma of incense, combining to heighten the experience for the worshippers. Each of these elements does its part to help the worshipper transcend the physical world and enter communion with the spiritual one.

As you visit Athens' churches, look for the following objects:

Iconostasis: An altar screen covered with curtains and icons divides the lay community from the priests—the material world from the spiritual one.

Cross: The Orthodox faith tends to use a Greek cross, with four equal arms (like a plus sign, sometimes inside a circle), which focuses on God's perfection (as opposed to the longer Latin cross, which more literally evokes the Crucifixion).

Icons: Unlike many Catholic church decorations, Orthodox icons (golden paintings of saints) are not intended to be lifelike. Packed with intricate symbolism and cast against a shimmering golden background, they're meant to remind viewers of the metaphysical nature of Jesus and the saints rather than their physical form, which is considered irrelevant.

Christ as *Pantocrator:* This image, so familiar to Orthodox Christians, shows Christ as King of the Universe, facing directly out, with penetrating eyes. Behind him is a halo divided by a cross, with only three visible arms—an Orthodox symbol for the Trinity (the fourth arm is hidden behind Christ).

cross, touching his thumb to his ring finger. This gesture forms the letters ICXC, the first and last letters of the Greek name for Jesus Christ (ΙΗΣΟΥΣ ΧΡΙΣΤΟΣ—traditionally C was substituted for Σ). Make the gesture yourself with your right hand. Touch the tip of your thumb to the tip of your ring finger and check it out: Your pinkie forms the I, your slightly crossed index and middle fingers are the X, and your thumb and ring finger make a double-C. Jesus Christ, that's clever. If you were a priest, you'd make the sign of the cross three times, to symbolize the Father, the Son, and the Holy Spirit.

The double-headed eagle that hangs around Damaskinos' neck is an important symbol of the Orthodox faith. It evokes the Byzantine Empire, during which Orthodox Christianity was at its peak as the state religion. Appropriately, the eagle's twin heads have a double meaning: The Byzantine Emperor was both the secular and spiritual leader of his realm, which exerted its influence over both East and West. (Historically, any power that wanted to be considered the successor of the ancient Roman Emperor—including the Holy Roman Empire and the Austro-Hungarian Empire—used this symbol.)

At the far end of the square from the cathedral is another statue, this one of a warrior holding a sword. This is **Emperor Constantine XI Palaeologus** (1404-1453), the final ruler of the Byzantine Empire (see photo on next page). He was killed defending Constantinople from the invading Ottomans, led by Mehmet the Conqueror. Considered the "last Greek king" and an unofficial saint, Constantine XI's death marked the ascension of the Ottomans as overlords of the Greeks for nearly four centuries. On his boots and above his head, you'll see the double-headed eagle again.

▶ *The small church tucked behind the right side of the cathedral is the...*

❽ Church of Agios Eleftherios

A favorite of local church connoisseurs, the late 12th-century Church of Agios Eleftherios (St. Eleutherius) is also known as Panaghia Ghorghoepikoos ("Virgin Mary, quick to answer prayers") and is sometimes referred to as "the old cathedral." It was used by the archbishops of Athens after the Ottomans evicted them from the church within the Parthenon. It's a jigsaw-puzzle hodgepodge of B.C. and A.D. adornments (and even tombstones) from earlier buildings. For example, the carved marble reliefs above the door were scavenged from the Ancient Agora in the 12th century. They are part of a calendar of ancient Athenian festivals, thought to

Constantine XI couldn't stop the Ottomans.

Agios Eleftherios church, with old stones.

have been carved in the second century A.D. The frieze running along the top of the building depicts a B.C. procession.

Later, Christians added their own symbols to the same panels, making the church a treasure trove of medieval symbolism. There are different kinds of crosses (Maltese, Latin, double) as well as carved rosettes, stars, flowers, and griffins feeding on plants and snakes. Walk around the entire exterior. Then step inside to sample unadorned 12th-century Orthodox simplicity.

▶ *Exit the church, go up to the main sidewalk level, and walk around to the back side of the church where you'll find a religious gear shop and the start of...*

❾ Agia Filotheis Street

This neighborhood is a hive of activity for Orthodox clerics. The priests dress all in black, wear beards, and don those fez-like hats. Despite their hermetic look, most priests are husbands, fathers, and well-educated pillars of the community, serving as counselors and spiritual guides to Athens' cosmopolitan populace.

Notice the stores. Just behind and facing the little church is the shop of the Theodoropoulos family—whose name manages to use nearly every Greek character available (ΘΕΟΔΩΡΟΠΟΥΛΟΣ). They've been tailoring priestly robes since 1907.

This is the first of many religious objects stores that line the street. Cross the busy Apollonos street and continue exploring the shops of Agia Filotheis street. The Orthodox religion comes with ample paraphernalia: icons, gold candelabras, hanging lamps, incense burners, oil lamps, chalices, various crosses, and gold objects worked in elaborate repoussé design.

Pop into the **stoa** (arcades) at #17 (on the left) to see workshops of the artisans who make these objects—painters creating or restoring icons in the traditional style, tailors making bishops' hats and robes, and carvers making little devotional statuettes.

A few more steps up on the left, the ➓ **Church of Agia Filotheis** (named, like the street, for a patron of Athens—St. Philothei) is adjacent to an office building (at #19) that serves as the headquarters for the Greek Orthodox Church. Athenians come here to file the paperwork to make their marriages (and divorces) official.

PART 3: ATHENS' "OLD TOWN" (THE PLAKA AND ANAFIOTIKA)

This part of our walk explores the atmospheric, twisty lanes of old Athens. Remember, back before Athens became Greece's capital in the early 1800s, the city was a small town of perhaps 10,000 residents, consisting of little more than what we'll see here.

▶ *Continue up Agia Filotheis street until you reach a tight five-way intersection. The street that runs ahead and to your right (labeled ΑΔΡIANOY—choked with souvenir stands and tourists—is our next destination. Look uphill and downhill along...*

➓ Adrianou Street

This intersection may be the geographical (if not atmospheric) center of the neighborhood called the Plaka. Touristy Adrianou street is a main pedestrian drag that cuts through the Plaka, running roughly east-west from Monastiraki to here. Adrianou offers the full gauntlet of Greek souvenirs: worry beads, sea sponges, olive products, icons, carpets, jewelry, sandals, faux vases and Greek statues, profane and tacky T-shirts, and on and on. It also offers plenty of cafés for tourists seeking a place to sit and rest their weary feet.

▶ *Bear left onto Adrianou and walk uphill several blocks. Finally, the street dead-ends at a T-intersection with Lysikratous street. (There's a small square ahead on the left, with palm trees, the Byzantine church of Agia Aikaterini, and an excavated area showing the street level 2,000 years ago.)*

From here you can turn right and take a few steps uphill to the Lysicrates Monument and Square (and skip ahead to the section on the

Adrianou—the Plaka's touristy main drag.

Hadrian's arch marks the Roman conquest.

Lysicrates Monument). But if you've got more time and stamina, it's worth a two-block walk to the left down Lysikratous street to reach the remains of the Arch of Hadrian.

⑫ Arch of Hadrian and Temple of Olympian Zeus

After the Romans conquered the Greeks, Roman emperor Hadrian (or Adrianos) became a major benefactor of the city of Athens. He built a triumphal arch, completed a temple beyond it (now ruined), and founded a library we'll see later. He also created a "new Athens" in the area beyond the arch (sometimes known as Hadrianopolis). The grand archway overlooks the bustling, modern Vasilissis Amalias avenue, facing the Plaka and Acropolis. (If you turned left and followed this road for 10 minutes, you'd end up back on Syntagma Square—where we began this walk.)

Arch of Hadrian

The arch's once-brilliant-white Pentelic marble is topped with Corinthian columns, the Greek style preferred by the Romans. Hadrian built it in A.D. 131 to celebrate the completion of the Temple of Olympian Zeus (which lies just beyond—described next). Like a big gate marking the entrance to a modern Chinatown, this arch represented the dividing line between the ancient city and Hadrian's new "Roman" city. An inscription on the west side informs the reader, "This is Athens, ancient city of Theseus," while the opposite frieze carries the message, "This is the city of Hadrian, and not of Theseus."

▶ *Look past the arch to see the huge (and I mean huge) Corinthian columns remaining from what was once a temple dedicated to the Olympian Zeus. For a closer look, cross the busy boulevard (crosswalk to the right). You can pretty much get the gist by looking through the fence. But to get close to those giant columns and wander the ruins, you can enter the site (covered by Acropolis combo-ticket—buy it here to avoid the Acropolis line). To reach the entrance (a five-minute walk), curl around the left side of the arch, then turn right (following the fence) up the intersecting street called Vasilissis Olgas. The entrance to the temple is a few minutes' walk up, on the right-hand side.*

Temple of Olympian Zeus (Olympieion)

This largest ancient temple in mainland Greece took almost 700 years to finish. It was begun late in the sixth century B.C. during the rule of the tyrant Peisistratos. He died before the temple was completed, and his successors were expelled from Athens. The temple lay abandoned, half-built, for centuries, until the Roman emperor Hadrian arrived to finish the job in A.D. 131. This must have been a big deal for Hadrian, as he came here in person to celebrate its inauguration. Romans did things big. When completed, the temple was 360 feet by 145 feet, consisting of two rows of 20 columns on each of the long sides and three rows of eight columns along each end (counting the corners twice). Although only 15 of the original 104 Corinthian columns remain standing, their sheer size (a towering 56 feet high) is enough to create a powerful impression of the temple's scale. The fallen column—which resembles a tipped-over stack of bottle caps—was toppled by a storm in 1852 (see photo, next page). The temple once housed a suitably oversized statue of Zeus, head of the Greek gods who lived on Mount Olympus, and an equally colossal statue of Hadrian.

▶ *Return to Lysikratous street and backtrack two blocks, continuing past the small square with the church you passed earlier. After another block, you'll run into another small, leafy square with the Acropolis rising behind it. In the square is an elegant, round, white-columned monument.*

⓭ Lysicrates Monument and Square

This elegant marble monument has Corinthian columns that support a dome that once held an ornamental vase on top. A frieze runs along the top, representing Dionysus turning pirates into dolphins. The monument is the sole survivor of many such monuments that once lined this ancient

At the Temple of Olympian Zeus, the Romans used Greek styles to build on a colossal scale.

"Street of the Tripods." It was so called because the monuments came with bronze tripods that displayed cauldrons (like those you'll see in the museums) as trophies. These ancient "Oscars" were awarded to winners of choral and theatrical competitions staged at the Theater of Dionysus on the southern side of the Acropolis. This now-lonely monument was erected in 334 B.C. by "Lysicrates of Kykyna, son of Lysitheides"—proud sponsor of the winning choral team that year. Excavations around the monument have uncovered the foundations of other monuments, which are now reburied under a layer of red sand and awaiting further study.

The square itself, shaded by trees, is a pleasant place to take a break before climbing the hill. Have a frappé or coffee at the café tables, grab a cheap cold drink from the cooler in the hole-in-the-wall grocery store to the left, or just sit for free on the benches under the trees.

▶ *From here you're only two blocks from the TI—you may want to detour there if you haven't stopped by yet (on pedestrian street leading to Acropolis Museum at Dionysiou Areopagitou 18). Otherwise, pass the Lysicrates Monument on its left-hand side, then head uphill toward the Acropolis, climbing the staircase called Epimenidou street. At the top of the stairs, turn right onto Stratonos street, which leads around the base of the Acropolis. As you walk along, the Acropolis and a row of olive trees are on your left. The sound of the crickets evokes for Athenians the black-and-white movies that were filmed in this area in the 1960s. To your right, you'll catch glimpses of another hill off in the distance.*

⑭ View of Lykavittos Hill

This cone-shaped hill (sometimes spelled "Lycabettus") topped with a tiny white church is the highest in Athens, at just over 900 feet above sea level.

Lysicrates Monument—an ancient "Oscar."

Lykavittos Hill, seen from the Acropolis.

The hill can be reached by a funicular, which leads up from the Kolonaki neighborhood to a restaurant, café, and view terrace at the top. Although it looms high over the cityscape, Lykavittos Hill will always be overshadowed by the hill you're climbing now.

▶ *At the small Church of St. George of the Rock (Agios Georgios, generally closed), go uphill, along the left fork. As you immerse yourself in a maze of tiny, whitewashed houses, follow signs that point to the Acropolis (even if the path seems impossibly narrow). This charming "village" is a neighborhood called...*

⑮ Anafiotika

These lanes and homes were built by people from the tiny Cycladic island of Anafi, who came to Athens looking for work after Greece gained its independence from the Ottomans. (Many stoneworkers and builders hired to construct the modern city of Athens built these higgledy-piggledy residences after-hours.) In this delightful spot, nestled beneath the walls of the Acropolis, the big city seems miles away. Keep following the Acropolis signs as you weave through narrow paths, lined with flowers and dotted with cats dozing peacefully in the sunshine (or slithering luxuriously past your legs). Though descendants of the original islanders still live here, Anafiotika (literally "little Anafi") is slowly becoming a place for wealthy locals to keep an "island cottage" in the city. As you wander through the oleanders, notice the male fig trees—no fruit—that keep away flies and mosquitoes. Smell the chicken-manure fertilizer (and cat poop), peek into delicate little yards, and enjoy the blue doors and maroon shutters...it's a transplanted Cycladic world. Posters of Anafi hang here and there, evoking the sandy beaches of the ancestral home island.

▶ *Follow the narrow walkway until you emerge from the maze of houses and hit a wider, cobbled lane. Turn right (downhill) and continue down the steep incline. When you hit a wider road (Theorias), turn left and walk toward the small, Byzantine-style Church of the Metamorphosis. (Note: To reach the Acropolis entry from here, you would continue along this road as it bends left around the hill.)*

Just before the church, turn right and go down the steep, narrow staircase (a lane called Klepsidras, labeled ΚΛΕΨΥΔΡΑΣ). You'll pass the first university of Athens (with a free little museum) on the right. Cross the street called Tholou and continue down Klepsidras. Enjoy the graffiti. The lane gets even narrower (yes, keep going between the plants).

The whitewashed settlement of Anafiotika, below the Acropolis, preserves a village ambience.

You'll pass a charming little café a block before you emerge at a railing overlooking some ruins.

⑯ The Roman Forum and the Tower of the Winds

The rows of columns framing this rectangular former piazza were built by the Romans, who conquered Greece around 150 B.C. and stayed for centuries. This square—sometimes called the "Roman Agora"—was the commercial center, or forum, of Roman Athens, with a colonnade providing shade for shoppers browsing the many stores that fronted it. Centuries later, the Ottomans made this their grand bazaar. The mosque was built upon a church that was built upon a Roman temple. The mosque, one of the oldest and best-preserved Ottoman structures, survives (although its minaret, like all minarets in town, was torn down by the Greeks when they won their independence from the Ottomans in the 19th century).

Take a few steps to the right to see the octagonal, domed **Tower of the Winds.** The carved reliefs depict winds as winged humans who fly in, bringing the weather. Built in the first century B.C., this building was an ingenious combination of clock, weathervane, and guide to the planets. The beautifully carved reliefs represent male personifications of the eight winds of Athens, with their names inscribed. As you walk down the hill (curving right, then left around the fence, always going downhill), you'll see reliefs depicting Lips, the southwest wind, holding a ship's steering rudder; Zephyros, the mild west wind, holding a basket of flowers; Skiron, scattering glowing coal from an inverted bronze brazier, indicating the warmer winter winds; and Boreas, the howling winter wind from the north, blowing a conch shell. The tower was once capped with a weathervane in the form of a bronze Triton (half-man, half-fish) that spun to indicate which wind

Roman Forum, heart of Roman Athens.

Tower of the Winds, with carved reliefs.

was blessing or cursing the city at the moment. Bronze rods (no longer visible) protruded from the walls and acted as sundials to indicate the time. And when the sun wasn't shining, people told time using the tower's sophisticated water clock, powered by water piped in from springs on the Acropolis. Much later, under Ottoman rule, dervishes used the tower as a place for their whirling worship and prayer.

▶ *It's possible but unnecessary to enter the ruins: You've seen just about everything from this vantage point. Don't confuse the Roman Forum with the older, more interesting Ancient Agora, which is near the end of this walk.*

Otherwise, from just below the Tower of the Winds, head to the right down Aiolou street one block to...

⑰ Agora Square (Plateia Agoras)

This leafy, restaurant-filled square is the touristy epicenter of the Plaka. On the left side of the square, you'll see the second-century A.D. ruins of the **⑱ Library of Hadrian** (open to the public). The four lone columns that sit atop the apse-like foundations are the remains of a fifth-century church. The ruins around it are all that's left of a big rectangular complex that once boasted 100 marble columns. Destroyed in the third century A.D., it was a cultural center (library, lecture halls, garden, and art gallery), built by the Greek-loving Roman emperor for the Athenian citizens. Notice how the excavated stones rest neatly in stacks awaiting funding for reconstruction.

▶ *Continue downhill alongside the ruins to the next block, where Aiolou intersects with the claustrophobic Pandrossou market street (which we walked along earlier). This crowded lane is worked by expert pickpockets—be careful. Look to the right up Pandrossou: You may see merchants sitting in folding chairs with their backs to one another, competition having soured their personal relationships. Turn left on Pandrossou and wade through the knee-deep tacky tourist souvenirs. Several shops here (including one we just passed on Aiolou, and two more on Pandrossou) supply fans of the "Round Goddess"—a.k.a. soccer (each team has its own store). Continue until you spill out into Monastiraki Square.*

⑲ Monastiraki Square Spin-Tour

We've made it from Syntagma Square—the center of urban Athens—to the city's *other* main square, Monastiraki Square, the gateway to the touristy

Old Town. To get oriented to Monastiraki Square, stand in the center, face the small church with the cross on top (which is north), and pan clockwise.

The name Monastiraki ("Little Monastery") refers to this square, the surrounding neighborhood, the flea-market action nearby...and the cute **Church of the Virgin** in the square's center (12th-century Byzantine, mostly restored with a much more modern bell tower).

Beyond that (straight ahead from the end of the square), **Athinas street** heads north to the Central Market, Omonia Square, and (after about a mile) the National Archaeological Museum.

Just to the right (behind the little church) is the head of **Ermou street**—the bustling shopping drag we walked down earlier (though no longer traffic-free here). If you turned right and walked straight up Ermou, you'd be back at Syntagma Square in 10 minutes.

Next (on the right, in front of the little church) comes Mitropoleos street—Athens' ⑳ **"Souvlaki Row."** Clogged with outdoor tables, this atmospheric lane is home to a string of restaurants that serve sausage-shaped, skewered meat—grilled up spicy and tasty. The place on the corner—Bairaktaris (ΜΠΑΪΡΑΚΤΑΡΗΣ)—is the best known, its walls lined with photos of famous politicians and artists who come here for souvlaki and pose with the owner. But the other two joints along here—Thanasis and Savvas—have a better reputation for their souvlaki. You can sit at the tables, or, for a really cheap meal, order a souvlaki to go for €2 (see listing in the Eating chapter.) A few blocks farther down Mitropoleos is the cathedral we visited earlier.

Continue spinning clockwise. Just past Pandrossou street (where you entered the square), you'll see a ㉑ **former mosque** (look for the Arabic script under the portico and over the wooden door). Known as the

Leafy Agora Square, lined with eateries.

Souvlaki Row—for a cheap, filling meal.

Tzami (from the Turkish word for "mosque"), this was a place of worship from the 15th to 19th century. Today it houses the Museum of Greek Folk Art's **ceramics collection.**

To the right of the mosque, behind the fence along Areos street, you might glimpse some huge Corinthian columns. This is the opposite end of the **Library of Hadrian** complex we saw earlier. Areos street stretches up toward the Acropolis. If you were to walk a block up this street, then turn right on Adrianou, you'd reach the ㉒ **Ancient Agora**—one of Athens' top ancient attractions (for more, take my ✪ Ancient Agora Tour or 🎧 download the free audio tour). Beyond the Agora are the delightful Thissio neighborhood, ancient Keramikos Cemetery, and Gazi district.

As you continue panning clockwise, next comes the pretty yellow building that houses the **Monastiraki Metro station.** This was Athens' original 19th-century train station—Neoclassical with a dash of Byzantium. This bustling Metro stop is the intersection of two lines: the old line 1 (green, with connections to the port of Piraeus, the Thissio neighborhood, and Victoria—near the National Archaeological Museum) and the modern line 3 (blue, with connections to Syntagma Square and the airport). The stands in front of the station sell seasonal fruit and are popular with commuters.

Just past the station, Ifestou street leads downhill into the ㉓ **flea market** (antiques, jewelry, cheap clothing, and so on—daily, best on Sun 8:00-15:00). If locals need a screw for an old lamp, they know they'll find it here.

Keep panning clockwise. Just beyond busy Ermou street (to the left of Athinas street, behind the A for Athens hotel—which has a rooftop bar popular for its views) is the happening **Psyrri** district. For years a run-down slum, this zone is being gentrified by twentysomethings with a grungy sense of style. Packed with cutting-edge bars, restaurants, cafés, and nightclubs, it may seem foreboding and ramshackle, but it is actually fun to explore.

㉔ Monastiraki Metro Station

Finish your walk by stepping into the Monastiraki Metro station and riding the escalator down to see an exposed bit of ancient Athens. Excavations for the Metro revealed an ancient aqueduct, which confined Athens' Eridanos River to a canal. The river had been a main axis of the town since the eighth century B.C. In the second century A.D., Hadrian and his engineers put a roof over it, turning it into a more efficient sewer. You're looking

Flea market chairs, for a well-deserved rest.

at Roman brick and classic Roman engineering. A cool mural shows the treasure trove archaeologists uncovered with the excavations.

This walk has taken us from ancient ruins to the Roman era, from medieval churches and mosques to the guerrilla fighters of Greek Independence, through the bustling bric-a-brac of the modern city, and finally to a place where Athens' infrastructure—both ancient and modern—mingles.

▶ *Our walk is over. If you're ready for a break, savor a spicy souvlaki on "Souvlaki Row." If you're looking for local color, head four blocks up Athinas street to the Central Market (described on page 130).*

Acropolis Tour

ΑΚΡΟΠΟΛΗ

Rising above the sprawl of Athens, the Acropolis ("high city") is a lasting testament to the glory of Greece's Golden Age. Even now, it's hard to overstate the historic and artistic importance of this place.

Its four major monuments—the Parthenon, Erechtheion, Propylaea, and Temple of Athena Nike—have survived remarkably well given the beating they've taken over the centuries. While the Persians, Ottomans, and Lord Elgin were cruel to the Acropolis in the past, it's now battling acid rain and pollution. Ongoing restoration means that you might see some scaffolding—but even that can't detract from the greatness of this sight.

Climbing Acropolis Hill and rambling its ruins, you'll feel like you've journeyed back in time to the birthplace of Western civilization itself.

ORIENTATION

Cost: €20 for Acropolis ticket, €10 off-season, €30 Acropolis combo-ticket also covers other major ancient sites—see page 123. If you buy an Acropolis combo-ticket at a different sight, you can bypass the ticket booth.

Hours: Daily May-Sept 8:00-20:00, April and Oct 8:00-19:00, Nov-March 8:00-15:00. Be aware that open hours are subject to change; check locally before planning your day.

Crowd-Beating Tips: Arrive early or late to avoid the crowds and midday heat. The place is miserably packed with tour groups from 10:00 to about 12:30 (when you might have to wait up to 45 minutes to get a ticket). On some days, as many as 6,000 cruise passengers converge on the Acropolis in a single morning. Buying an Acropolis combo-ticket at another sight may save ticket-buying time, but doesn't ensure a speedy entry: The worst lines are caused by the bottleneck of people trying to squeeze into the site through the Propylaea gate. Late in the day, as the sun goes down, the white Parthenon stone gleams a creamy golden brown, and what had been a tourist war zone is suddenly peaceful. On my last visit, I showed up late and had the place to myself in the cool of early evening.

Getting There: There's no way to reach the Acropolis without a lot of climbing (though wheelchair users can take an elevator). Figure a 10- to 20-minute hike from the base of the Acropolis up to the hilltop archaeological site. There are multiple paths up to the Acropolis, but the only ticket office and site entrance are at the western end of the hill (to the right as you face the Acropolis from the Plaka).

If you're touring the Ancient Agora, you can hike directly up to the Acropolis entrance along the Panathenaic Way. The approach from the Dionysiou Areopagitou pedestrian zone behind (south of) the Acropolis is slightly steeper. From this walkway, various well-marked paths funnel visitors up to the entrance; the least steep one climbs up from the parking lot at the western end of the pedestrian zone. You can reach this path either by taxi or by tourist train (the Athens Happy Train—see page 172), but note that it still involves quite a bit of uphill hiking.

If you use a wheelchair, you can take the elevator that ascends the Acropolis (from the ticket booth, go around the left side of the hilltop). However, once you are up top, the site is not particularly level or well-paved, so you may need help navigating the steep inclines and uneven terrain.

Information: Supplement this tour with the free information brochure (you may have to ask for it when you buy your ticket) and info plaques posted throughout; tel. 210-321-4172, www.culture.gr.

Tours: You can hire your own tour guide at the entrance, but I wouldn't—the guides here tend to be rude, overpriced, and underqualified.

🎧 Download my free Acropolis audio tour. This sight is particularly suited to an audio tour, as it allows your eyes to enjoy the wonders of the Acropolis while your ears learn its story.

Length of This Tour: Allow two hours.

Baggage Check: Backpacks are allowed; baby strollers are not. There's a checkroom just below the ticket booth near Mars Hill.

Services: There are WCs at the Acropolis ticket booth and more WCs and drinking fountains atop the Acropolis, in the former museum building (behind the Parthenon). Also inside the turnstiles are machines selling cheap, cold bottles of water. Picnicking is not allowed on the premises. Near the ticket booth are a juice/snack stand, a drinking fountain, a post office, and a museum shop.

Plan Ahead: Wear sensible shoes—Acropolis paths are steep and uneven. In summer, it gets very hot on top, so take a hat, sunscreen, sunglasses, and a bottle of water.

Starring: The Parthenon and other monuments from the Golden Age, plus great views of Athens and beyond.

Acropolis Overview

STANDING RUINS
ORIGINAL FOOTPRINT

To Ancient Agora

To Monastiraki

ANAFIOTIKA

Mars Hill

THEORIAS

To Plaka

ELEVATOR

ERECHTHEION

ACROPOLIS FLAG

BEULÉ GATE

PROPYLAEA

TICKETS

STRATONOS

To Plaka

ACROPOLIS ENTRANCE

TEMPLE OF ATHENA NIKE

PARTHENON

THESPIDOS

EPIMENIDOU

THRASSILOU

To Apostolou Pavlou & Thissio

ODEON OF HERODES ATTICUS

THEATER OF DIONYSUS

GARIVALDI

PROPYLEON

ERECHTHIOU

PARTHENONOS

DIONYSIOU AREOPAGITOU

ROVERTOU GALLI

BUS PARKING LOT

Filopappos Hill

MAKRIGIANNI

KALLISPERI

100 Meters

100 Yards

ACROPOLIS MUSEUM

Akropoli

BACKGROUND

The Acropolis has been the heart of Athens since the beginning of record-ed time (Neolithic era, 6800 B.C.). This limestone plateau, faced with sheer, 100-foot cliffs and fed by permanent springs, was a natural fortress. The Mycenaeans (c. 1400 B.C.) ruled the area from their palace on this hilltop, and Athena—the patron goddess of the city—has been worshipped here since around 800 B.C.

But everything changed in 480 B.C., when Persia invaded Greece for the second time. As the Persians approached, the Athenians evacu-ated the city, abandoning it to be looted and vandalized. All of the temples atop the Acropolis were burned to the ground. The Athenians fought back

The Acropolis' sheer cliffs have made it a natural fortress since the beginning of time.

at sea, winning an improbable naval victory at the Battle of Salamis. The Persians were driven out of Greece, and Athens found itself suddenly victorious. Cash poured into Athens from the other Greek city-states, which were eager to be allied with the winning side.

By 450 B.C., Athens was at the peak of its power and the treasury was flush with money...but in the city center, the Acropolis still lay empty, a vast blank canvas. Athens' leader at the time, Pericles, was ambitious and farsighted. He funneled Athens' newfound wealth into a massive rebuilding program. Led by the visionary architect/sculptor Pheidias (490-430 B.C.), the Athenians transformed the Acropolis into a complex of supersized, ornate temples worthy of the city's protector, Athena.

The Parthenon, Erechtheion, Propylaea, and Temple of Athena Nike were built as a coherent ensemble (c. 450-400 B.C.). Unlike most ancient sites, which have layer upon layer of ruins from different periods, the Acropolis we see today was started and finished within two generations— a snapshot of the Golden Age set in stone.

The Acropolis

Mars Hill

To Ancient Agora,
Monastiraki & Plaka

Cliffs

THEORIAS

WALL

PROPYLAEA

STANDING RUINS

ORIGINAL FOOTPRINT

BEULÉ
GATE

TICKETS, WC &
JUICE/SNACKS

ACROPOLIS
ENTRANCE

TEMPLE
OF
ATHENA
NIKE

ODEON
OF
HERODES
ATTICUS

❶ Odeon of Herodes
Atticus
❷ Propylaea
(Entrance Gate)
❸ Temple of Athena Nike
❹ Monument of Agrippa
❺ Beulé Gate
❻ Statue of Athena
Promachos
❼ Parthenon
❽ Porch of the Caryatids
❾ Erechtheion
❿ Greek Flag
⓫ Views of Athens (2)

To
Apostolou Pavlou
& Thissio

To
Acropolis
Museum

DIONYSIOU AREOPAGITOU

THE TOUR BEGINS

▶ *Climb up to the Acropolis ticket booth and the site entrance, located at
the west end of the hill.*

Near this entrance (below and toward the Ancient Agora) is the huge, crag-
gy boulder of **Mars Hill** (a.k.a. Areopagus). Consider climbing this rock for
great views of the Acropolis' ancient entry gate, the Propylaea (described
later) and the Ancient Agora. Mars Hill's bare, polished rock is extremely

slippery—a metal staircase to the left helps somewhat. (For more on Mars Hill and its role in Christian history, see page 122.)

Before you show your ticket and enter the Acropolis site, make sure you have everything you'll need for your visit. Remember, after you enter the site, there are no services except WCs and water fountains.

▶ *Enter the site, and start climbing the paths that switchback up the hill, following signs on this one-way tourist route (bearing to the right). Before you reach the summit, peel off to the right for a bird's-eye view of the...*

Propylaea entrance, as seen from Mars Hill.   Odeon theater, for ancients and moderns.

❶ Odeon of Herodes Atticus

The grand Odeon huddles under the majestic Propylaea. Tourists call it a "theater," but Greeks know it's technically an odeon, as it was mainly used for musical rather than theatrical performances. (Odeon—like the English word "ode"—comes from the Greek word for "song.").

A large 5,000-seat amphitheater built during Roman times, it's still used for performances. From this perch you get a good look at the stage setup: a three-quarter-circle orchestra (where musicians and actors performed in Greek-style theater), the overgrown remnants of a raised stage (for actors in the Roman tradition), and an intact stage wall for the backdrop. Originally it had a wood-and-tile roof as well.

The Odeon is sometimes called the Herodion, after Herodes Atticus, a wealthy landowner who had the building erected in A.D. 161 in memory of his wife. Herodes Atticus was a Greek with Roman citizenship, a legendary orator, and a friend of Emperor Hadrian. This amphitheater is the most famous of the many impressive buildings he financed around the country.

Destroyed by the invading Herulians a century after it was built, the Odeon was reconstructed in the 1950s to the spectacular state it's in today. It's open to the public only during performances, such as the annual Athens & Epidavros Festival, when an international lineup of dance, music, and theater is performed beneath the stars. If there's something on tonight, you may see a rehearsal from here. Athenians shudder when visitors—recalling the famous "Yanni Live at the Acropolis" concert—call this stately place "Yanni's Theater."

▶ *After climbing a few steps, you'll see two gates: On the right, steps lead down to the Theater of Dionysus (described on page 124); on the left is the actual entry uphill into the Acropolis. Stay left and continue up to reach the grand entrance gate of the Acropolis: the Propylaea. Stand at the foot of the (very) steep marble staircase, facing up toward the big Doric columns.*

As you face the Propylaea, to your left is a tall, gray stone pedestal with nothing on it: the Monument of Agrippa. On your right, atop the wall, is the Temple of Athena Nike. Behind you stands a doorway in a wall, known as the Beulé Gate.

❷ The Propylaea

The entrance to the Acropolis couldn't be through just any old gate; it had to be the grandest gate ever built. Ancient visitors would stand here, catching their breath before the final push to the summit, and admire these gleaming columns and steep steps that almost fill your field of vision. Imagine the psychological impact this awe-inspiring, colonnaded entryway to the sacred rock must have had on ancient Athenians. The odd mix of stairs here shows how the way up looked in different eras. The original ascent, a ramp that allowed sacrificial animals to make the climb, was replaced with a grand marble staircase in Hellenistic times, and then with a zigzag road (partly still intact) in the Middle Ages. (A few original stairs survive under the wooden ramp.)

The Propylaea (pro-PEE-leh-ah) is U-shaped, with a large central hallway (the six Doric columns), flanked by side wings that reach out to embrace the visitor. The central building looked like a mini-Parthenon, with Doric columns topped by a triangular pediment. Originally, the Propylaea was painted bright colors.

The left wing of the Propylaea was the Pinakotheke, or "painting

Climbing the Propylaea's staircase.

Temple of Nike, overlooking the Propylaea.

gallery." In ancient times, this space contained artwork and housed visiting dignitaries and VIPs.

The buildings of the Acropolis were all built to complement one another. The Propylaea was constructed in five short years (437-432 B.C.), just after the Parthenon was finished. Its design (by Mnesicles) was meant to give the visitor a hint of the Parthenon to come. Both buildings are Doric (with Ionic touches) and are aligned east-west, with columns of similar width-to-height ratios.

▶ *Before ascending, notice the monuments flanking the entryway. To the right of the Propylaea, look up high atop the block wall to find the...*

❸ Temple of Athena Nike

The Temple of Athena Nike (Greeks pronounce it "NEEK-ee") was started as the Propylaea was being finished (c. 427-421/415 B.C.). It was designed by Callicrates, one of the architects of the Parthenon. This little temple— nearly square, 11 feet tall, with four columns at both ends—had delightful proportions. Where the Parthenon and Propylaea are sturdy Doric, this temple pioneered the Ionic style in Athens, with elegant scroll-topped columns.

The Acropolis was mainly dedicated to the goddess Athena, patron of the city. At this temple, she was worshipped for bringing the Athenians victory ("Nike"). A statue of Athena inside the temple celebrated the turning-point victory over the Persians at the Battle of Plataea in 479 B.C. It was also meant to help ensure future victory over the Spartans in the ongoing Peloponnesian War. The statue was never given wings because Athenians wanted Athena to stay and protect their city—hence the place became known as the Temple of Wingless Athena.

The Temple of Athena Nike has undergone extensive restoration. From 2001 to 2010, it was completely disassembled, then cleaned, shored up, and pieced back together. This was the third time in its 2,500-year history that the temple had been entirely taken apart. The Ottomans pulled it down at the end of the 17th century and used the stone elsewhere, but Greeks reassembled the temple after regaining their independence. In 1935, it was taken apart for renovation and put back together in 1939. Unfortunately, that shoddy work did more harm than good—prompting the most recent restoration. Now it's been done the right way and should hold for another 2,500 years.

▶ *To the left (as you face the Propylaea) is the...*

The Monument of Agrippa once held grand statues of Athens' heroes and rulers.

❹ Monument of Agrippa

This 25-foot-high pedestal, made of big blocks of gray marble with yellow veins, reaches as high up as the Temple of Athena Nike. The (now-empty) pedestal once held a bronze statue of the four-horse chariot owned by Eumenes II, king of Pergamon—the winner of the race at the 178 B.C. Panathenaic Games.

Over the centuries, each ruler of Athens wanted to put his mark on the mighty Acropolis. When Rome occupied the city, Marc Antony placed a statue of himself and his girlfriend Cleopatra atop the pedestal. After their defeat, the Roman general Agrippa (son-in-law of Augustus) replaced it with a statue of himself (in 27 B.C.).

▶ Before entering, look downhill. Behind you is the...

❺ Beulé Gate

This ceremonial doorway was built by the Romans, who used the rubble from buildings that had recently been destroyed in the barbarian Herulian invasion of A.D. 267. (The gate's French name comes from the archaeologist who discovered it in 1852.) During Roman times, this gate was the official entrance to the Acropolis, making the Propylaea entry even grander.

▶ Climb the steps (or today's switchback ramps for tourists) and go...

Inside the Propylaea

Imagine being part of the grand parade of the Panathenaic Festival, held every four years (see page 83). The procession started at Athens' city gate (near the Keramikos Cemetery), passed through the Agora, then went around Mars Hill, through the central hall of the Propylaea, and up to the

Roman-built Beulé Gate.

Stackable column drum, in the Propylaea.

glorious buildings atop the summit of the Acropolis. Ancient Greeks approached the Propylaea by proceeding straight up a ramp in the middle, which narrowed as they ascended, funneling them into the central passageway. There were five doorways into the Propylaea, one between each of the six columns.

The Propylaea's central hall was once a roofed passageway. The marble-tile ceiling, now partially restored, was painted sky blue and studded with stars. Floral designs decorated other parts of the building. The interior columns are Ionic, a bit thinner than the Doric columns of the exterior. You'll pass by some big column drums with square holes in the center, where iron pins once held the drums in place. (Greek columns were not usually made from a single piece of stone, but from sections—"column drums"—stacked on top of one another.)

▶ *Pass through the Propylaea. As you emerge out the other end, you're on top of the Acropolis. There it is—the Parthenon! Just like in the books (except for the scaffolding). Stand and take it all in.*

The Acropolis
The "Acropolis rock" is a mostly flat limestone ridge covering seven acres, scattered with ruins. There's the Parthenon ahead to the right. To the left of that, with the six lady pillars (Caryatids), is the Erechtheion. The Panathenaic Way ran between them. The processional street and the buildings were aligned east-west, like the hill.

Ancient visitors here would have come face-to-face with a welcoming 30-foot ❻ **Statue of Athena Promachos,** which stood between the Propylaea and the Erechtheion. (Today there's just a field of rubble, the statue's former location marked by three stones forming a low wall.) This was one of three statues of Athena on the Acropolis. The patron of the city was worshipped for her wisdom, purity, and strength; here she appeared in her role as "Frontline Soldier" *(promachos),* carrying a shield and spear. The statue was cast by Pheidias, the visionary sculptor/architect most responsible for the design of the Acropolis complex. The bronze statue was so tall that the shining tip of Athena's spear was visible from ships at sea. The statue disappeared in ancient times, and no one knows its fate.

Two important buildings, now entirely gone, flanked this statue and the Panathenaic Way. On the right was the Chalkotheke, a practical storage area for the most precious gifts brought to the temple—those made of copper and bronze. On the left stood the Arrephorion, a house where young virgins called *ergastinai* worked at looms to weave the *peplos,* the sacred dress given to Athena on her birthday.

▶ *Move a little closer for the classic view of the* ❼ *Parthenon.*

Parthenon—West End

The Parthenon is the hill's showstopper—the finest temple in the ancient world, standing on the highest point of the Acropolis, 490 feet above sea level. It's now largely in ruins, partly from the ravages of time, but mostly from a direct mortar-shell hit sustained in 1687 (launched by a Venetian army aiming for the gunpowder stored inside by the Ottomans).

It's impressive enough today, but imagine how awesome the Parthenon must have looked when it was completed nearly 2,500 years ago (much of the west end is behind scaffolding for now—if it's still up during your visit, circle around to the east side). This is Greece's largest Doric temple: 228 feet long and 101 feet wide. At each end were 8 outer and 6 inner fluted Doric columns, with 17 columns along each side, plus 23 inner columns in the Doric and 4 in the Ionic style. The outer columns are 34

For 2,000 years, the Parthenon's west end has greeted visitors.

feet high and 6 feet in diameter. In its heyday, the temple was decorated with statues and carved reliefs, all painted in vivid colors. It's considered Greece's greatest Doric temple—but not its purest example because it incorporates Ionic columns and sculpture.

The Parthenon served the cult of Virgin Athena. It functioned as both a temple (with a cult statue inside) and as the treasury of Athens (safeguarding the city's funds, which included the treasury of the Athenian League).

This large temple was completed in less than a decade (c. 447-438 B.C.), though the sculptural decoration took a few years more (finished c. 432). The project's overall "look" was supervised by the master sculptor-architect Pheidias, built by well-known architects Ictinus and Callicrates, and decorated with carved scenes from Greek mythology by sculptors Agoracritos and Alcamenes.

It's big, sure. But what makes the Parthenon truly exceptional is that the architects used a whole bagful of optical illusions to give the building an ever-so-subtle feeling of balance, strength, and harmonious beauty. Architects know that a long, flat baseline on a building looks to the human eye like it's sagging, and that parallel columns appear to bend away from each other. To create a building that looked harmonious, the Parthenon's ancient architects calculated bends in the construction. The base of the Parthenon actually arches several inches upward in the middle to counteract the "sagging" illusion. Its columns tilt ever so slightly inward (one of the reasons why the Parthenon has withstood earthquakes so well). If you extended all the columns upward several miles, they'd eventually touch. The corner columns are thicker to make them appear the same size as the rest; they're also spaced more closely. And the columns bulge imperceptibly halfway up (an effect called "entasis"), giving the subconscious impression of stout, barrel-chested men bearing the weight of the roof. For a building that seems at first to be all about right angles, the Parthenon is amazingly short on straight, structural lines.

All these clever refinements form a powerful subconscious impression on the viewer that brings an otherwise boring architectural box to life. It's amazing to think that all this was planned and implemented in stone so long ago.

The statues and carved reliefs that once decorated the outside of the Parthenon are now mostly faded or missing, but a few remain. Look up at the crossbeam atop the eight columns, decorated with panels of relief carvings called metopes, depicting Athenians battling Amazons.

PEDIMENT

CROSSBEAM

TRIGLYPHS

METOPES

CAPITAL
(DORIC)

FRIEZE
(TUCKED
UNDERNEATH
ATOP INNER
COLUMNS)

COLUMN

FLUTING

Find the pediment (triangle roofline), metopes (on the crossbeam), and frieze (inner crossbeam).

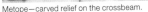
Metope—carved relief on the crossbeam.

Pediment statues depict Athena's triumph.

Originally there were 92 Doric-style metopes in high relief, mostly designed by Pheidias himself.

The crossbeams once supported a triangular pediment (now gone). This area was once filled in with statues, showing Athena with her olive tree competing with Poseidon and his trident to be Athens' patron god. Today just one statue remains (and it's a reconstruction).

Approach closer and look between the eight columns. Inside, there's another row of eight columns, supporting a covered entrance porch. Look up above the inner eight columns. Decorating those crossbeams are more relief carvings—the "frieze." Originally a 525-foot-long frieze of panels circled the entire building. It showed the Panathenaic parade—women, men on horseback, musicians, sacrificial animals being led to the slaughter—while the gods looked on. All of the sculptures—metopes, pediment, and frieze—were originally painted in bright colors.

Today, most of the originals are in museums across Europe. In the early 1800s, the cream of the crop, the famous Elgin Marbles (you'd better call them the Parthenon Marbles in Greece), were taken by Lord Elgin to England, where they now sit in the British Museum. The Acropolis Museum (which stands at the base of the hill—you'll see it from a distance later on this tour) was built to house the fragments of the Parthenon sculpture that Athens still owns...and to try to entice the rest back from London.

▶ *Continue along the Panathenaic Way, walking along the long left (north) side of the Parthenon.*

Parthenon—North Side

This view of the Parthenon gives you a glimpse into how the temple was constructed and how it is being reconstructed today by modern archaeologists.

Looking between the columns, you can see remnants of the interior walls, built with thousands of rectangular blocks. The columns formed an open-air porch around the main building, which had an entry hall and *cella* (inner sanctum). Large marble roof tiles were fitted together atop wooden beams. These tiles were carved so thin that the interior glowed with the light that shone through it.

The Parthenon's columns are in the Doric style—stout, lightly fluted, with no base. The simple capital on top consists of a convex plate topped with a square slab. The capitals alone weigh eight to nine tons. The cross-beams consist of a lower half ("architrave") and an upper half, its metopes interspersed with a pattern of grooves (called triglyphs).

The Parthenon (along with the other Acropolis buildings) was constructed from the very finest materials, including high-quality, white Pentelic marble from Penteliko Mountain, 16 miles away. Unlike the grand structures of the Egyptians (pyramids) and the Romans (Colosseum), the Parthenon was built not by slaves but by free men who drew a salary (though it's possible that slaves worked at the quarries).

Imagine the engineering problems of quarrying and transporting

Devotees once entered at the east end.

more than 100,000 tons of marble. Most likely the column drums (five to ten tons each) were cut at the quarry and rolled here. To hoist the drums in place, the builders used four-poster cranes (and Greek mathematics), centering the drums with a cedar peg in the middle. The drums were held together by metal pins that were coated in lead to prevent corrosion, then fitted into a square hole cut in the center of the drum. (The Ottomans scavenged much of this lead to make bullets, contributing to the destruction of the temple over the ages.) Because the Parthenon's dimensions are not mathematically precise (intentionally so), each piece had to be individually cut and sized to fit its exact place. The Parthenon's stones are so well-crafted that they fit together within a thousandth of an inch. The total cost to build the Parthenon (in today's dollars) has been estimated at over a billion dollars.

▶ Continue on to the...

Parthenon—East End (and Entrance)

This end was the original entrance to the temple. Over the doorway, the triangular pediment depicted the central event in Athenian history—the birth of Athena, their patron goddess. Today, the pediment barely survives, and the original statues of the gods are partly in the British Museum. Originally, the gods were gathered at a banquet (see a copy of the reclining Dionysus at the far left—looking so drunk he's afraid to come down). Zeus got a headache and asked Hephaistos to relieve it. As the other gods looked on in astonishment, Hephaistos split Zeus' head open, and—at the peak of the pediment—out rose Athena. The now-missing statues were surprisingly realistic and three-dimensional, with perfect anatomy and bulging muscles showing through transparent robes.

Imagine this spot during the age of Pericles and Socrates. Stand back far enough to take it all in, imagine the huge statue of Athena that once stood inside, and picture the place in all its glory on the day of the Panathenaic parade. The procession would have traveled through the Agora, ascended the Acropolis, passed through the Propylaea, and arrived here at the altar of Athena in front of the entrance of the Parthenon. People gathered on the surrounding grass (the hard stone you see today was once covered with plants). Musicians played flutes and harps, young women carried gifts, and men on horseback reined in their restless animals. On open-air altars, the priests offered a sacrifice of 100 oxen (a hecatomb—the ultimate sacrificial gift) to the goddess Athena.

After the Golden Age: The Acropolis Through History

Classical: The Parthenon and the rest of the Acropolis' buildings survived through classical times largely intact, despite Herulian looting (A.D. 267). As the Roman Empire declined, precious items were carried off, including the 40-foot Athena statue.

Christian: After nearly a thousand years as Athena's temple, the Parthenon became a Christian church (fifth century A.D.). Pagan sculptures and decorations were removed (or renamed), and the interior was decorated with colorful Christian frescoes. The west end of the building became the main entrance, and the interior was reconfigured with an apse at the east end.

Muslim: In 1456, the Turks arrived and converted the Parthenon into a mosque, adding a minaret. The Propylaea entry gate was used as a palace for the Turkish ruler of Athens. The Turks also used the Parthenon to store gunpowder, unfortunately leading to the greatest catastrophe in the Acropolis' long history.

1687: A Venetian army laid siege to the Acropolis. The Venetians didn't

Here at the Parthenon entrance, a select few celebrants were chosen to go inside. They proceeded up the steps, passed through the majestic columns into the foyer *(pronaos)*, and entered the main hall, the *cella*—100 feet long, 60 feet wide, and 4 stories tall. At the far end of the room stood an enormous, 40-foot-tall statue of Athena Parthenos (Athena the Virgin). This was a chryselephantine statue, meaning "of gold and ivory"—from the Greek *chrysos*, "gold," and *elephantinos*, "ivory." Its wooden core was plated with ivory to represent her skin and a ton of pure gold to define her garments (or so say local guides). Dressed as a warrior, care about ancient architecture. As far as they were concerned, it was a lucky hit of mortar fire that triggered the massive explosion that ripped the center out of the Parthenon, rattled the Propylaea and the other buildings, and wiped out the Turkish defenders.

Lord Elgin: In 1801, Lord Elgin, the British Ambassador to the Ottomans in Constantinople, got "permission" from the sultan to gather

sculptures from the Parthenon, buy them from locals, and even saw them off the building. He carted half of them to London. Although a few original frieze, metope, and pediment carvings still adorn the Parthenon, most of the sculptures are on display in museums, including the Acropolis Museum.

From Independence to the Present: In the 19th century, newly independent Greece tore down the Parthenon's minaret and the other post-Classical buildings atop the Acropolis, turning it into an archaeological zone. Since then, the place has been excavated and there have been several renovation efforts.

she wore a helmet and rested her shield at her side. Her image was reflected in a pool in the center of the room. (The pool also served a practical purpose—the humidity helped preserve the ivory treasures.) In Athena's left hand was a spear propped on the ground. In her upturned right hand was a statuette of Nike—she literally held Victory in the palm of her hand.

The statue—the work of the master Pheidias—was either carried off in A.D. 426 to Constantinople, where it subsequently vanished, or was burned by the Herulians in A.D. 267. (A small-scale Roman copy is on display in Athens' National Archaeological Museum; see page 111.) Another famous chryselephantine statue by Pheidias—of a seated Zeus—was considered one of the Seven Wonders of the Ancient World.

The culmination of the Great Panathenaic parade every four years was the presentation of a newly woven *peplos* to Athena. The dress was intended for the life-size wooden statue of Athena kept at the Erechtheion (described later). But during the Grand Panathenaia (every four years), the Athenians presented a huge robe—big enough to cover a basketball court—to the 40-foot Virgin Athena in the Parthenon.

▶ *The modern brown-brick building behind you once housed the former Acropolis museum—its collection has been painstakingly moved into the modern Acropolis Museum down the hill. The old museum building may reopen someday as a coffee shop, but for now, it has just WCs and a drinking fountain alongside.*

   Across the street from the Parthenon stands the Erechtheion, where the Panathenaic parade ended. There were three entrances to this building: the famous Porch of the Caryatids (the six ladies), the north porch (behind the Erechtheion), and the east end (to the right of the caryatids). Start by enjoying its famous...

❽ Porch of the Caryatids

An inspired piece of architecture, this balcony has six beautiful maidens functioning as columns that support the roof. Each of the lady-columns has a base beneath her feet, pleated robes as the fluting, and a fruit-basket hat as the capital. Both feminine and functional, they pose gracefully, exposing a hint of leg—a combination of architectural elements and sculpture.

These are faithful copies of the originals, five of which are on display in the Acropolis Museum. The sixth was removed (c. 1805) by the sticky-fingered Lord Elgin, who shipped it to London. The Caryatids were supposedly modeled on *Karyatides*—women from Karyai (modern Karyes, near Sparta on the Peloponnese), famous for their upright posture and noble character.

The Erechtheion (c. 421-406 B.C.) is sometimes ascribed to Mnesicles, the man who designed the Propylaea. Whereas the Propylaea and Parthenon are both sturdy Doric, the Erechtheion is elegant Ionic. In its day, it was a stunning white building (of Pentelic marble) with painted capitals and a frieze of white relief on a darker blue-gray background.

Near the porch (below, to the left) is an olive tree, a replacement for the one Athena planted here in her face-off with Poseidon (described later). Olive trees have been called "the gift of Athena to Athens." Greece has more than 140 million of these trees.

Erechtheion's caryatids—these stone maidens support the roof of this prestigious temple.

▶ *Walk around to the right and view the Erechtheion from the east end, with its six Ionic columns in a row.*

❾ Erechtheion

Though overshadowed by the more impressive Parthenon, the Erechtheion (a.k.a. Erechtheum) was perhaps more prestigious. It stood on one of the oldest sites on the hill, where the Mycenaeans had built their palace. (It lay mainly on the south side, facing the Parthenon, under the huge scattered stones—all that's left of the seventh-century Athena Temple.) Inside the Erechtheion was a life-size, olive-wood statue of Athena in her role of Athena Polias ("Protector of the City"). Pericles took the statue with him when the Athenians evacuated their city to avoid the invading Persians. Dating from about 900 B.C., this statue, much older and more venerable than either of Pheidias' colossal statues, supposedly dropped from the sky as a gift from Athena.

This unique, two-story structure fits nicely into the slope of the hill. The east end (with the six Ionic columns) was the upper-level entrance. The lower entrance was on the north side (on the right), 10 feet lower, where you see six more Ionic columns. (These columns are the "face of the Acropolis" that Athenians see from the Plaka.) The Porch of the Caryatids is attached to the south side of the building. Looking inside the temple, you can make out that the inner worship hall, the *cella,* is divided in two by walls.

This complex layout accommodated the worship of various gods who had been venerated here since the beginning of time. Legend says this was the spot where Athena and Poseidon fought for naming rights to the city. Poseidon threw his trident, which opened a gash in the earth to

The Erechtheion sits atop temple ruins.

Greece's flag flies proudly above the city.

bring forth water. It left a diagonal crack that you can still see in the pavement of the entrance farthest from the Parthenon (although lightning is a more likely culprit). But Athena won the contest by stabbing a rock with her spear, sprouting an olive tree near the Porch of the Caryatids. The twin *cellas* of the Erechtheion allowed the worship of both gods—Athena and Poseidon—side by side to show that they were still friends.

▶ *Look to the right (beyond the Plaka-facing porch). The modern elevator carries people with limited mobility up to the Acropolis. The north wall of the Acropolis has a retaining wall built from column drums. This is about all that remains of an earlier half-finished Parthenon that was destroyed after the Persian invasion of 480 B.C. The Persians razed the entire Acropolis, including an unfinished temple then under construction. The Athenians rebuilt as fast as they could with the scattered material to fortify the city against Sparta.*

Walk to the far end of the Acropolis. There you'll find an observation platform with a giant...

⑩ Greek Flag

The blue-and-white Greek flag's nine stripes symbolize the nine syllables of the Greek phrase for "Freedom or Death." That phrase took on new meaning when the Nazis entered Athens in April of 1941. According to an oft-repeated (but unverified) story, the evzone (elite member of a select infantry unit) guarding the flag flying here was ordered by the Nazis to remove it. He calmly took it down, wrapped himself in it...and jumped to his death. About a month later, two heroic teenagers, Manolis Glezos and Apostolis Santas, scaled the wall, took down the Nazi flag, and raised the Greek flag. This was one of the first well-known acts of resistance against the Nazis, and the boys' bravery is honored by a plaque near the base of the steps. To this day, Greeks can see this flag from just about anywhere in Athens and think of their hard-won independence.

▶ *Walk out to the end of the rectangular promontory to see the...*

⑪ View of Athens

The Ancient Agora spreads below the Acropolis, and the sprawl of modern Athens whitewashes the surrounding hills. In 1830, the population of Athens' core was about 5,000. By 1900, it was 600,000, and during the 1920s, with the influx of Greeks from Turkey, the population surged to 1.5 million. The city's expansion could barely keep up with its exploding

View of Lykavittos Hill.

South view of the Temple of Olympian Zeus.

population. With the boom times in the 1950s and 1980s, the city grew to nearly four million. Pan around. From this perch, you're looking at the homes of one out of every three Greeks.

Looking down on the **Plaka,** find (looking left to right) the Ancient Agora, with the Temple of Hephaistos. Next comes the Roman Forum (the four columns and palm trees) with its round, white, domed Temple of the Winds monument. The **Anafiotika** neighborhood clings to the Acropolis hillside directly below us. About eight blocks beyond that, find the dome of the cathedral.

Lykavittos Hill, Athens' highest point, is crowned with the Chapel of St. George (and an expensive view restaurant; cable car up the hill). Looking farther in the distance, you'll see lighter-colored bits on the mountains behind—these are **Pentelic quarries,** the source of the marble used to build (and now restore) the monuments of the Acropolis.

As you continue panning to the right, you'll spot the beige Neoclassical **Parliament** building, marking Syntagma Square; the **National Garden** is behind and to the right of it. In the garden is the yellow **Zappeion,** an exhibition hall. The green area in the far distance contains the 60,000-seat, marble **Panathenaic Stadium**—an ancient venue (on the site where Golden Age Athens held its games), which was rehabbed in 1896 to help revive the modern Olympics.

▶ *Complete your visual tour of Athens at the south edge of the Acropolis. To reach the viewpoint, walk back toward the Parthenon, then circle along its left side, by the cliff-top wall. Belly up to that wall for...*

More Views of Athens

Look to the left. In the near distance are the huge columns of the **Temple of Olympian Zeus.** Begun in the sixth century B.C., it wasn't finished until the time of the Roman emperor Hadrian, 700 years later. It was the biggest temple in all of Greece, with 104 Corinthian pillars, housing a 40-foot seated statue of Zeus, a replica of the famous one created by Pheidias in Olympia. This area was part of Hadrian's "new Athens," a planned community in his day, complete with the triumphal **Arch of Hadrian** near the temple.

The **Theater of Dionysus**—which hosted great productions (including works by Sophocles) during the Golden Age—lies in ruins at your feet. For more on the theater, see page 124.

Beyond the theater is the wonderful **Acropolis Museum,** a black-and-gray modern glass building, with three rectangular floors stacked at irregular angles atop each other. The top floor, which houses replicas and some originals of the Parthenon's art, is angled to match the orientation of that great temple.

Looking right, you see **Filopappos Hill**—the green, tree-dotted hill topped with a marble funerary monument to a popular Roman senator, Philopappos, who died in the early second century. This hill is where the Venetians launched the infamous mortar attack of 1687 that destroyed the Parthenon. Today, a theater here hosts popular folk-dancing performances (see page 171).

Farther in the distance, you get a glimpse of the turquoise waters of the **Aegean** (the only island visible is Aegina). While the Persians were burning the Acropolis to the ground, the Athenians watched from their ships as they prepared to defeat their foes in the history-changing Battle of Salamis. In the distance, far to the right, is the port of Piraeus (the main departure point for boats to the islands).

▶ *Our tour is finished. Enjoy a few final moments with the Acropolis before you leave. If you're not yet ready to return to modern Athens, you can continue your sightseeing at several nearby sights.*

To reach the Theater of Dionysus ruins and the Acropolis Museum: Head left when you exit the Acropolis site, and walk down to the Dionysiou Areopagitou pedestrian boulevard. Turn left and follow this walkway along the base of the Acropolis. You'll pass (on the left) the Theater of Dionysus ruins, and (on the right) the Acropolis Museum (see the ✪ Acropolis Museum Tour chapter).

To reach the Ancient Agora: Turn right as you exit the Acropolis site, pass Mars Hill, and follow the Panathenaic Way down to the Ancient Agora (possible to enter through the "back door," facing the Acropolis). My Ancient Agora Tour is covered in the next chapter and is also available as 🎧 a free audio tour.

The ruins of the Theater of Dionysus, which once staged works by Sophocles.

Ancient Agora Tour
ΑΡΧΑΙΑ ΑΓΟΡΑ

While the Acropolis was the ceremonial showpiece, it was the Agora that was the real heart of ancient Athens. For some 800 years, from its founding in the sixth century B.C. to its destruction by barbarians in A.D. 267, the Agora (which means "gathering place") was the hub of all commercial, political, and social life in Athens, as well as home to much of its religious activity. Everybody who was anybody in ancient Athens spent time here, from Socrates and Plato to a visiting missionary named Paul. Little survives from the classical Agora. Other than one very well-preserved temple and a rebuilt stoa, it's a field of humble ruins. But that makes it a quiet, uncrowded spot to wander and get a feel for the ancients.

ORIENTATION

Cost: €8 or covered by €30 Acropolis combo-ticket (which you can buy here; see page 123).

Hours: Daily May-Sept 8:00-20:00, April and Oct 8:00-19:00, Nov-March 8:00-15:00. The Agora Museum inside has the same hours, except on Monday, when it opens at 11:00.

Getting There: From the Monastiraki Metro stop, walk a block south (up-hill, toward the Acropolis). Turn right on Adrianou street, and follow the pedestrian-only, café-lined street along the railroad tracks for about 200 yards. The Agora entrance is on your left, across from a small, yellow church. The entrance can be hard to spot: It's where a path crosses over the railroad tracks (look for a small, pale-yellow sign that says *Ministry of Culture—Ancient Agora*).

Compass Points: The Agora entrance is north; the Acropolis is south.

Information: Panels with printed descriptions of the ruins are scattered helpfully throughout the site; tel. 210-321-0180, www.culture.gr.

Tours: ∩ Download my free Ancient Agora audio tour.

Cuisine Art: Picnicking is not allowed in the Agora. Plenty of cafés and tavernas line busy Adrianou street near the Agora entrance, and more good eateries front the Apostolou Pavlou pedestrian walkway that hems in the western edge of the Agora, in the district called Thissio (see the Eating chapter).

Starring: A well-preserved temple, a rebuilt stoa, three monumental statues, and the ruins of the civilization that built the Western world.

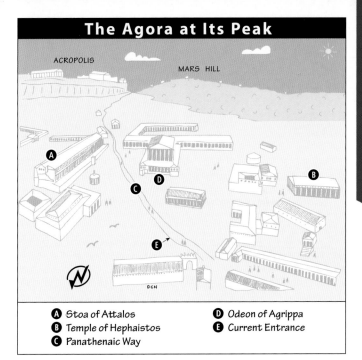

The Agora at Its Peak

ACROPOLIS

MARS HILL

Ⓐ Stoa of Attalos
Ⓑ Temple of Hephaistos
Ⓒ Panathenaic Way
Ⓓ Odeon of Agrippa
Ⓔ Current Entrance

THE TOUR BEGINS

Entering the site from Adrianou street, belly up to the illustration at the top of the ramp that shows the Athenian Agora at the peak of its size. Face the Acropolis (to the south), look out over the expanse of ruins and trees, and get oriented.

The long column-lined building to the left is the reconstructed Stoa of Attalos (#13 on the illustration). To your right, atop a hill (the view is likely blocked by trees) is the well-preserved Temple of Hephaistos (#20). The pathway called the Panathenaic Way (#21) runs from the Agora's entrance up to the Acropolis. Directly ahead of you are three tall statue-columns

Panathenaic Way cutting through the Agora.   Statue-columns amid the greenery.

(also probably obscured by trees)—part of what was once the Odeon of Agrippa (#12).

In the distance, the Agora's far end is bordered by hills. From left to right are the Acropolis (#1), the Areopagus ("Hill of Ares," or Mars Hill, #2), and Pnyx Hill (#3).

Although the illustration implies that you're standing somewhere behind the Stoa Poikile ("Painted Stoa," #28), in fact you are located in front of it, closer to the heart of the Agora, to the left of the Altar of the Twelve Gods (#26). In ancient times, that altar was considered the geographical center of Athens, from which distances were measured. Today, the area north of the altar (and north of today's illustration) remains largely unexcavated and inaccessible to tourists, taken over by the railroad tracks and Adrianou street.

This self-guided tour starts at the Stoa of Attalos (with its museum), then crosses the Agora to the Temple of Hephaistos, returning to the Panathenaic Way via three giant statues. Finally, we'll head up the Panathenaic Way toward the Acropolis.

▶ *Walk to the bottom of the ramp at your left for a better view. Find a shady spot to ponder...*

❶ The Agora

What lies before you now is a maze of ruins—the remains of many centuries of buildings.

A millennium before the time of Socrates, during the Mycenaean Period (around 1600-1200 B.C.), this area held the oldest cemetery in Athens. Later, the Agora was developed into a political forum—the center for speeches, political announcements, and demonstrations. The

Ancient Agora

30 Meters
30 Yards

STANDING RUINS
ONLY FOUNDATIONS

TOUR ENDS

To Plaka, Mars Hill
& Acropolis

STOA OF
ATTALOS

PANATHENAIC WAY

WC

To Apostolou
Pavlou
Entrance

AGORA
←ILLUSTRATION

TEMPLE OF
HEPHAISTOS

MAIN
ENTRANCE

TICKETS

ADRIANOU

To Monastiraki
Square &

MONASTIRAKI

To Ermou Street
& Psyrri District

TOUR BEGINS

To Thissio

❶ Agora	❻ Great Drain	⓫ Panathenaic Way
❷ Stoa of Attalos	❼ Tholos	⓬ Post-Herulian Wall
❸ Agora Museum	❽ Temple of Hephaistos	⓭ Church of the
❹ Middle Stoa	❾ Statue of Hadrian	Holy Apostles
❺ Corinthian Capital	❿ Odeon of Agrippa	⓮ South Gate

rectangular area (about 100 yards by 200 yards, bordered by hills) naturally evolved into a marketplace, with sellers lured by the crowds. Over time, that central square became surrounded by buildings, then filled in with more buildings. There were stoas like the (reconstructed) Stoa of Attalos (above on the left), used for shops and offices; temples such as the Temple of Hephaistos; and government buildings. Imagine the square framed by these buildings—decorated with painted statues and friezes, fronted with columns of gleaming white marble, topped with red-tile roofs. The square itself was studded with trees and dotted with statues, fountains, and altars. Merchants sold goods from wooden market stalls.

The square buzzed with people—mostly men and lower-class working women, as the place was considered a bit vulgar for genteel matrons. Both men and women would be dressed in simple tunics (men's were knee-length, women's to the ankle). The Agora was the place to shop—to buy clothes, dishes, or to get your wagon wheel fixed. When a perishable product was available—for example, a catch of fresh fish—a certain bell was rung to announce its arrival. If you needed a zoning permit for your business, you came to the courthouse. You could make an offering to the gods at a number of temples and altars. At night, people attended plays and concerts, and nearby tavernas hummed with excited drinkers. Many people passed through here on their way to somewhere else, as this was the main intersection in town (and ancient Athens probably had a population of at least 100,000). On holidays, the procession ran down main street, the Panathenaic Way. At any time, this was the place to come to run into your friends, to engage in high-minded discussion with philosophers such as Socrates or Diogenes, or just to chat and hang out.

▶ *Now go to the long, intact, colonnaded building on your left (entrance at the south/far end).*

❷ Stoa of Attalos

This stoa—an ancient shopping mall—was originally built by the Greek-loving King Attalos II of Pergamon (in modern-day Turkey, 159-138 B.C.) as a thank-you gift for the education he'd received in Athens. That structure is long gone, and the building we see today is a faithful reconstruction built in the 1950s by the American School of Classical Studies.

This is a typical two-story stoa. Like many of the Agora's buildings, it's made of white Pentelic and gray-blue Hymettus marble from the quarries northeast of the city. The portico is supported on the ground floor by 45 Doric columns (outer layer) and 22 Ionic columns (inner layer). The upper story uses Ionic columns. This mix of Doric and Ionic was typical of buildings from the period.

Stoas, with their covered walkways, provided protection from sun and rain for shoppers and merchants. This one likely served as a commercial mall. The ground floor was divided by walls into 21 rooms that served as shops (it's now the museum). Upstairs were offices (which today house

Stoa of Attalos—reconstructed "mall."

The stoa now houses the Agora Museum.

more of the Agora Museum and research facilities of the American School of Classical Studies).

Like malls of today, the Agora's stoas were social magnets. Imagine ancient Greeks (their hard labor being done by slaves and servants) lounging here, enjoying the shade of the portico. The design of the pillars encourages people to lean against them (just as you may be doing right now)—with fluting starting only above six feet for the comfort of philosophers.

▶ Inside, the Stoa of Attalos houses the...

❸ Agora Museum

This excellent little museum displays some choice rubble that helps bring the place to life. Before entering, enjoy the arcade. Near the fifth column, find the impressive sculpted head of a bearded man with a full head of hair. This Head of a Triton (c. A.D. 150) comes from one of the statues that decorated the Odeon of Agrippa. Three of his fellow statues are still standing (we'll see them soon).

Walk halfway down the arcade and step inside the museum (included with your Agora ticket). Its modest but engaging collection fills a single long hall and part of the next level up. Look in the corner for the 1952 photo showing this spot before the reconstruction. This well-described chronological stroll through art from 3200 B.C. gives you a glimpse of life in ancient Athens. Along the hall on the left, big panels show the Agora and Acropolis during each age, allowing you to follow their physical evolution.

The first few cases show off jars from various eras, including Neolithic (when the Agora was first inhabited) and Geometric (1050-700 B.C.). Much of this exhibit shows how Greek pottery evolved over time. Pottery was a popular export product for the seafaring Greeks. The earliest pottery

An ancient commode.

Clay ballot voting Aristides out of Athens.

featured geometric patterns, then came floral and animal motifs, and finally painted human silhouettes—first showing black figures on the natural orange clay, then red figures on a black background. In case 26, look for the cute little baby's commode, with a photo showing how it was used.

Cases 30-32 (on right) hold items from early democracy. The "voting machine" (*kleroterion,* case 31) was used to choose judges. Citizens put their name in the slots, then black and white balls went into the tube to randomly select who would serve. Below are bronze ballots from the fourth century. The pottery shards with names painted on them (*ostrakan,* case 30) were used as ballots in voting to ostracize someone accused of corruption or tyranny. Find the ones marked ΘΕΜΙSΘOΚLES NEOKLEOS (item #37) and ARISSTEIΔES (item #17). During the Golden Age, Themistocles and Aristides were rivals (in both politics and romance) who served Athens honorably, but were exiled in political power struggles.

In case 32, see the *klepsydra* ("water thief")—a water clock used to time speeches at Council meetings. It took six minutes for the 1.7 gallons to drain out. A gifted orator truly was good to the last drop...but not a second longer.

Across the hall (under the banner, between cases 68 and 67) is the so-called "Stele of Democracy" (c. 336 B.C.). This stone monument is inscribed with a decree outlawing tyranny. Above, a relief carving shows Lady Democracy crowning a man representing the Athenian people.

Next to that (in case 67) is a bronze shield captured from defeated Spartans in the tide-turning Battle of Sphacteria, which gave Athens the upper hand in the first phase of the Peloponnesian War.

In the middle of the room, find the case of coins. These drachms and tetradrachms feature Athena with her helmet. In Golden Age times, a drachm was roughly a day's wage. The ancients put coins like these in the mouth of a deceased person as payment for the underworld ferryman Charon to carry the soul safely across the River Styx. Coin #7, with the owl, was a four-drachm piece; that same owl is on Greece's €1 coin today.

▶ *Exiting the museum at the far end of the arcade (where there's a WC and a water fountain), backtrack to the southern end of the stoa (where you entered), then cross the main road and continue straight (west) along the lane, across the middle of the Agora. You're walking alongside the vast ruins (on your left) of what once was the...*

❹ Middle Stoa

Stretching clear across the Agora, this was part of a large complex of what were likely shops and office buildings. It was a long, narrow rectangle (about 500 by 60 feet), similar to the reconstructed Stoa of Attalos you just left. You can still see the two lines of stubby column fragments that once supported the roof, a few stone steps, and (at the far end) some of the reddish foundation blocks. Constructed around 180 B.C., this stoa occupied what had been open space in the center of the Agora.

▶ *Midway down the lane (near the wooden ramp), you'll come across a huge and frilly upper cap, or capital, of a column.*

❺ Corinthian Capital

This capital (dating from the fourth century B.C.) once stood here atop a colossal column, one of a dozen columns that lined the monumental entrance to the Odeon of Agrippa, a theater that extended northward from the Middle Stoa. (We'll learn more about the Odeon later.) The capital's elaborate acanthus-leaf decoration is a nice example of the late Corinthian style. Rarely used in Greek buildings, the Corinthian style became wildly popular with the Romans.

From here look back toward the entrance, overlooking what was once the vacant expanse at the center of the Agora. In 400 B.C., there was no Middle Stoa and no Odeon—this was all open space. As Athens grew, the space was increasingly filled in with shops and monuments.

▶ *Continue westward across the Agora. Near the end of the Middle Stoa, you'll see a gray well—still in its original spot and worn by the grooves of ropes. From here look up at the Acropolis, where the towering but empty pedestal once sported the Monument of Agrippa, a grand statue with four horses. Mars Hill, likely topped with tourists, is where the Apostle*

This leaf-ornamented Corinthian capital once topped a column at the Roman-built Odeon.

Paul famously preached the Gospel (described on page 122). Below the Erechtheion are broken columns shoring up the side of the hill. These were rubble from temples that were destroyed by the Persians. Just beyond the well to the right is a big drain and a round foundation—the tholos. Backtrack from the well a few steps to cross the wooden ramp, and go left to find the ditch that was once part of the...

❻ Great Drain

Dug in the fifth century B.C. and still functioning today, these ditches channel rainwater runoff from the southern hills through the Agora. Here at the southwest corner of the Agora, two main collection ditches meet and join. You can see exposed parts of the stone-lined ditch. The well we just passed was also part of this system.

▶ *Passing across the ditch and through the line of shrubbery, take the left fork toward a 60-foot-across round footprint with a stubby column in its center. This is the...*

❼ Tholos

This rotunda-shaped building was an assembly place for the administrators of Athens' City Council. Built around 465 B.C., it originally had six inner Ionic columns that held up a conical roof. In the middle was an altar (marked today by the broken column).

The fundamental unit of Athenian democracy was the Assembly, made up of the thousands of adult male citizens who could vote. Athenian citizens were organized into 10 tribes; in order to prevent the people living in any one geographical area from becoming dominant, each tribe was composed of citizens from city, coastal, and inland areas. Each man in the Assembly was considered to be from one of these tribes.

All of Athens' governing bodies met in the Agora. Though some Assembly meetings were held in the Agora's main square, the main assemblies took place just uphill, on the slope of Pnyx Hill. The City Council also met in the Agora. The Council consisted of 500 men (50 from each of the 10 tribes) who were chosen from the Assembly by lottery to serve a one-year term. The Council proposed and debated legislation, but because Athens practiced direct (not representational) democracy, all laws eventually had to be approved by the whole Assembly. The Council chose 50 ministers who ran the day-to-day affairs.

As part of the civic center complex, the *tholos* served several functions. It was the headquarters, offices, and meeting hall for the 50 administrators. Many lived and ate here, since the law required that at least a third of these ministers be on the premises at all times (they served for terms of only 36 days). The *tholos* also housed the city's official weights and measures. Any shopper in the Agora could use these to check whether a butcher or tailor was shortchanging them. As the center of government, the *tholos* of any ancient Greek city was also a kind of temple. The altar in the middle held an eternal flame, representing the hearth of the extended "family" that was Athens.

▶ *Beyond and above the tholos is the hill-capping Temple of Hephaistos. To reach it, climb the stairs to the left and go through the trees, pausing along the way at a viewpoint with a chart.*

❽ Temple of Hephaistos

One of the best-preserved and most typical of all Greek temples, this is textbook Golden Age architecture. Started in 450 B.C.—just before the Parthenon—it was built at Athens' peak as part of the massive reconstruction of the Agora after invading Persians destroyed the city (480 B.C.). But the temple wasn't completed and dedicated until 415 B.C., as work stalled when the Greeks started erecting the great buildings of the Acropolis. Notice how the frieze around the outside of the building was only decorated on the side facing the Agora (it's blank on the other three sides, as were most temples of this kind—the Parthenon is unusual for its continuous, wrap-around frieze).

This is classic "peristyle" temple (like the Parthenon), meaning that the building is surrounded by columns—six on each end, 13 on the long sides (counting the corners twice). Also like the Parthenon, it's made of Pentelic marble in the Doric style, part of Pericles' vision of harking back to Athens' austere, solid roots. But the Temple of Hephaistos is only about half the size of the grand Parthenon and with fewer refinements (compared to the Parthenon's elaborate carvings and fancy math).

The temple's entrance was on the east end, facing the Agora. Priests would enter through the six columns here, crossing through a covered portico (note the coffered ceiling) and a three-sided alcove, called the *pronaos* or "pre-temple," before reaching the central hall *(cella)*. Large bronze statues of Hephaistos, the blacksmith god, and Athena, patroness of Athens and of arts and crafts, once stood in this central hall. In ancient times, metalworking and pottery shops surrounded the temple, but in the third century B.C. some were replaced with gardens, similar to today's. Behind the *cella* (the west end) is another three-sided alcove, matching the *pronaos*.

The carved reliefs (frieze and metopes) that run around the upper part of the building are only partly done; some panels may have been left unfinished.

The well-preserved Temple of Hephaistos.

Frieze of centaurs battling humans.

At the end overlooking the Agora, look between the six columns and up at the frieze above the *pronaos* to find scenes of the mythical hero Theseus battling his enemies, trying to unite Athens. Theseus would go on to free Athens from the dominance of Crete by slaying the bull-headed Minotaur. The frieze decorations led Athenians to mistakenly believe that the temple once held the remains of Theseus—and to this day, they call it the Theseion.

Walk around behind the temple, to the far (west) end. The frieze above the three-sided alcove depicts the mythological battle between the Lapith tribe and centaurs during a wedding feast. Other scenes you'll see around the building (there are many interpretations) include Hercules (his labors and deification) and the birth of Erichthonios (one of Athens' first kings, who was born when spurned Hephaistos tried to rape Athena, spilled semen, and instead impregnated Gaia, the earth).

In the seventh century A.D., the temple was converted into the Church of Agios Georgios and given the vaulted ceiling that survives today. During the Ottoman occupation, the Turks kept the church open but permitted services to be held only once each year (on St. George's Day). Because it was continually in use, the temple-turned-church is remarkably well-preserved—but notice the bullet holes, damage sustained mostly in the 1820s, when the Greeks resisted the Turks.

▶ *Note that there's a "back door" exit nearby for those wanting to take the smooth, paved walkway up to the Acropolis, rather than the rough climb above the Agora. (To find the exit, face the back of the temple, turn right, and follow the path to the green gate, which deposits you on the inviting, café-lined Apostolou Pavlou pedestrian drag. From here you could turn left and walk up toward the Acropolis.)*

But there's still more to see in the Agora. Wind your way down the hill (northeast) and find the headless...

❾ Statue of Hadrian

The first Roman emperor to wear a beard (previously a Greek fashion), Hadrian (r. A.D. 117-138) was a Grecophile and benefactor of Athens. Get close to this second-century A.D. statue and notice the insignia on the breastplate. There's Romulus and Remus, being suckled by the she-wolf who supports Athena on her back. This was Hadrian's vision—that by conquering Greece, Rome actually saved it. Hadrian was nicknamed Graecula ("The Little Greek") for his love of Greek philosophy, literature,

Roman emperor Hadrian loved Greek culture.

Triton fronting the Odeon of Agrippa.

and a handsome Greek teenager named Antinous. Hadrian personally visited Athens, where he financed a comprehensive building program, including the Arch of Hadrian, Library of Hadrian, Temple of Olympian Zeus (which had been started by the Greeks), and a whole new master-planned neighborhood. (For more on these sights, see the ✪ Athens City Walk chapter or 🎧 download my free audio tour.) Hadrian's legacy endures. The main street through the Plaka is now called Adrianou—"Hadrian's" street.

▶ *Continuing on, head straight down the lane (to the left of Hadrian) and you'll pass three giants on four pedestals, which once guarded the...*

⑩ Odeon of Agrippa

This theater/concert hall (a.k.a. the "Palace of the Giants"), once fronted by a line of six fierce Triton and Giant statues, was the centerpiece of the Agora during the Roman era.

A plaque explains the history of this building: During the Golden Age, this site was simply open space in the very center of the Agora. The *odeon* (a venue designed mainly for musical performances) was built by the Roman general and governor Marcus Agrippa in the time of Caesar Augustus (around 15 B.C.), when Greece was a Roman-controlled province. For the theater-loving Greeks and their Greek-culture-loving masters, the *odeon* was a popular place. Two stories tall and built into the natural slope of the hill, it could seat more than a thousand people.

Back then, the entrance was on the south side (near the Middle Stoa), and these Triton and Giant statues didn't yet exist. Patrons entered from the south, walking through two rows of monumental columns, topped by Corinthian capitals. After the lobby, they emerged at the top row of a 20-tier, bowl-shaped auditorium, looking down on an orchestra and stage paved with multicolored marble and decorated with statues. The sightlines were great because the roof, spanning 82 feet, had no internal support columns. One can only assume that, in its heyday, the *odeon* hosted concerts, poetry readings, and more lowbrow Roman-oriented entertainment.

Around A.D. 150, the famously unsupported roof collapsed. By then, Athens had a bigger, better performance venue (the Odeon of Herodes Atticus, on the other side of the Acropolis—see page 48), so the Odeon of Agrippa was rebuilt at half the size as a 500-seat lecture hall. The new entrance was here on the north side, fronted by six colossal statues serving as pillars. Only two Tritons (with fish tails), a Giant (with a snake's tail), and an empty pedestal remain.

The building was burned to the ground in the Herulian invasion of A.D. 267 (explained later, under "Post-Herulian Wall"). Around A.D. 400, a large palace was built here, which also served as the university (or "gymnasium," which comes from the Greek word for "naked"—young men exercised in the buff during PE here). It lasted until the Constantinople-based Emperor Justinian closed all the pagan schools in A.D. 529. A plaque under the first statue gives more information.

▶ *Continue to the main road, where you'll see we've made a loop. Now turn right and start up toward the Acropolis on the...*

⑪ Panathenaic Way

The Panathenaic Way was Athens' main street. It started at the main city gate (the Dipylon Gate, near the Keramikos Cemetery), cut diagonally through the Agora's main square, and wound up to the Acropolis—two-thirds of a mile in all. The Panathenaic Way was the primary north-south road, and here in the Agora it intersected with the main east-west road to the port of Piraeus. Though some stretches were paved, most of it (then as now) was just packed gravel. It was lined with important temples, businesses, and legal buildings.

During the Panathenaic Festival, held in the summer, this was the main parade route. Every four years on Athena's birthday, Greeks celebrated by giving her statue a new dress, called a *peplos*. A wheeled float carrying the *peplos* was pushed up this street. Thousands participated—some on horseback, others just walking—while spectators watched from wooden grandstands erected along the way. When the parade reached the Acropolis, the new dress was ceremonially presented to Athena and

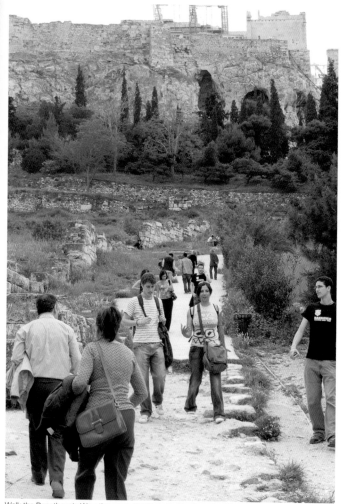

Walk the Panathenaic Way, the same street strolled by Socrates, Plato, and today's tourists.

used to adorn her life-size statue at the Erechtheion. Today's tourists use the same path to connect the Agora and the Acropolis.

▶ *Continue up the Panathenaic Way, past the Stoa of Attalos. Along the left-hand side are several crude walls and column fragments.*

⑫ Post-Herulian Wall

This wall marks the beginning of the end of Roman Athens.

In A.D. 267, the barbarian Herulians sailed down from the Black Sea and utterly devastated Athens. (The crumbling Roman Empire was helpless to protect its provinces.) The Herulians burned most of the Agora's buildings to the ground, leaving it in ashes.

As soon as the Herulians left, the surviving Athenians began hastily throwing up this wall—cobbled together from rubble—to keep future invaders at bay. They used anything they could find: rocks, broken columns, statues, frieze fragments, all thrown together without mortar to make a wall 30 feet high and 10 feet thick. Archaeologists recognize pieces scavenged from destroyed buildings, such as the Stoa of Attalos and the Odeon of Agrippa.

Up until this point, the Agora had always been rebuilt after invasions (such as the Persians in 480 B.C. and Romans in 89 B.C.); but after the Herulians, the Agora never recovered as a public space. What remained suffered through a Slavic invasion in A.D. 580. By A.D. 700, it was a virtual ghost town.

▶ *Next came the Christians. On the right is the...*

⑬ Church of the Holy Apostles

This charming little church with the lantern-like dome marks the Agora's revival. Built around A.D. 1000, it commemorates St. Paul's teaching in the

Post-Herulian wall to keep barbarians out.

Holy Apostles church adds a Christian layer.

Agora (see information about Mars Hill on page 122). Under protection from the Christian rulers of Byzantium (in Constantinople, modern-day Istanbul), Athens—and the Agora—slowly recovered from centuries of invasions and neglect. The church was built on the ruins of an ancient nymphaeum, or temple atop a sacred spring, and became one of many Christian churches that served the booming populace of Byzantine Athens.

This church was the prototype for later Athenian churches: a Greek-cross floor plan with four equal arms, topped by a dome and featuring windows with tall horseshoe-shaped arches. (The narthex, or entrance, was added later, spoiling the four equal arms.)

Enter (if the church is open) around the far side. It contains some interesting 17th-century Byzantine-style frescoes. The windows are in flower and diamond shapes. From the center, look up at Jesus as *Pantocrator* ("ruler over all") at the top of the dome, and see the icon on the altar and the faded frescoes on the walls. Notice the remains of the marble altar screen with wide-open spaces—frames that once held icons.

▶ *Our tour is over. There are three exits: the gate through which you entered, at Adrianou street; the "back door" gate behind the Temple of Hephaistos; and the* ⑭ **south gate** *next to the Church of the Holy Apostles. To go to the Acropolis, exit through the gate by the church and head straight up the hill.*

Acropolis Museum Tour
ΜΟΥΣΕΙΟ ΑΚΡΟΠΟΛΗΣ

Athens' Acropolis Museum, opened in 2009, was custom-built to show-case artifacts from the Acropolis—the Parthenon sculptures, the original caryatids from the Erechtheion, and much more—complemented by modern exhibits about the Acropolis. The state-of-the-art building that houses the collection is the boldest symbol yet of today's Athens.

The museum also serves as a sort of 21st-century Trojan horse, intended to lure the famous Parthenon sculptures (the Elgin Marbles) away from London's British Museum and back to Athens. So far, Britain has refused to give in, for fear of setting a precedent...and getting "me, too" notices from Italy, Egypt, Iran, Iraq, and other nations wanting to reclaim the missing pieces of their cultural heritage.

ORIENTATION

Cost: €5.

Hours: Mon 8:00-16:00, Tue-Sun 8:00-20:00, Fri until 22:00.

Getting There: It's the giant modern building facing the south side of the Acropolis from across the broad Dionysiou Areopagitou pedestrian drag. The museum is next to the Akropoli Metro stop on Makrigianni, a street lined with restaurants.

Information: Museum guards (with red badges) can answer questions, and a 13-minute video plays continuously in the atrium (level 3); tel. 210-900-0900, www.theacropolismuseum.gr.

Length of This Tour: Allow 1.5 hours.

Baggage Check: There's a free bag check at the counter near the turn-stiles at the base of the ramp (required for big bags).

Photography: No photos are allowed on the ground floor (level 0) or of the Archaic statues on level 1. It's OK to take photos without flash in the rest of the museum.

Services: A café and gift shop are on the ground floor (level 0); level 2 has a pricey but good restaurant, a bookstore, and great views.

Starring: Marble masterpieces from one of the most influential archaeological sites in human history.

THE TOUR BEGINS

Even as it echoes the ancient history all around it, the Acropolis Museum's striking, glassy building—designed by Swiss-born, New York-based architect Bernard Tschumi—gives a postmodern jolt to Athens' otherwise staid, mid-century-concrete cityscape. Its two lower levels are aligned with the foundations of ancient ruins discovered beneath the building (which are exposed and still being excavated). The top floor sits askew, imitating the orientation of the Parthenon. A long terrace extends over the main entry, with café tables stretching toward panoramic views of the Acropolis. The museum's glass walls maximize the natural light inside the building and also "disappear," focusing attention on the statuary and views of the Acropolis itself.

Visitors enter into a grand lobby. The ground floor (level 0) has the ticket office, WCs, museum shop, and temporary exhibits. To proceed chronologically through the exhibits, you'd start with the Archaic collection on level 1, then go upstairs (to the top floor—level 3) for the Parthenon section, then back down to level 1 for Hellenistic and Roman sculpture. But for this tour, we'll do the small Hellenistic and Roman section as an out-of-chronological-sequence side-trip from the Archaic and Classical sections, and let the top-floor Parthenon sculptures be our finale.

▸ *After going through the turnstiles, head up the long, glass...*

Ramp

Pause to look through the glass floor at the ancient ruins being excavated beneath the museum. The major buildings of ancient Athens were at the Acropolis and Agora—this was a neighborhood of everyday houses and shops. Appropriately, the ramp is lined with artifacts that were found in the sanctuaries and houses on the slopes leading up to the Parthenon. Many of these artifacts, dating from the fourth millennium B.C. to the fifth-century A.D., owe their well-preserved state to having been buried with their owners.

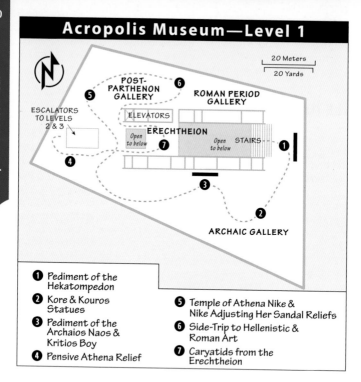

Acropolis Museum—Level 1

20 Meters

20 Yards

POST-PARTHENON GALLERY

ROMAN PERIOD GALLERY

ESCALATORS TO LEVELS 2 & 3

ELEVATORS

ERECHTHEION

Open to below

STAIRS

Open to below

ARCHAIC GALLERY

❶ Pediment of the Hekatompedon

❷ Kore & Kouros Statues

❸ Pediment of the Archaios Naos & Kritios Boy

❹ Pensive Athena Relief

❺ Temple of Athena Nike & Nike Adjusting Her Sandal Reliefs

❻ Side-Trip to Hellenistic & Roman Art

❼ Caryatids from the Erechtheion

Among the ramp's highlights is case #5 (on the left), which takes you step by step through marriage rituals in ancient Athens. Freestanding cases midramp give insight into the similarities between ancient Greek pagan worship rituals and later Christian styles. One has Christian-looking votives thanking the gods for prayers answered. On the right, just below the stairs, is an offering box (like you see in churches today); this one stood at the Sanctuary of Aphrodite. To assure a good marriage, you'd have been wise to pop in a silver drachma.

Level 1

▶ *Climb the stairs at the top of the ramp toward a collection of statues.*

❶ Pediment of the Hekatompedon (570 B.C.)

Throughout the centuries, three temples of Athena have occupied the spot where the Parthenon stands today. The fragments assembled here, from 570 B.C., once adorned the Hekatompedon ("100 feet"), the first of those temples. The still-under-construction building was leveled by invading Persians in 480 B.C., paving the way for the Parthenon to be built. On the left, Hercules fights the sea monster Triton. In the center are the scant remains of two lions killing a bull. On the left is Hercules struggling with a sea snake. To the right is a three-headed demon with a snake tail. Each figure holds an object in its hand, representing the elements of wind, water, and fire. While their expressions are more goofy than demonic, they illustrate the struggle of man versus nature. Traces of the original paint are still apparent.

▶ *Turn right and enter a gallery flooded with daylight.*

❷ Kore and Kouros Statues

In this column-lined gallery stand several kore (female) and kouros (male) statues. They sport the characteristic stiff poses, braided hair, generic faces, and mysterious smiles of the Archaic era (c. 700-480 B.C.). For more on Archaic statues, see page 108.

The men are generally naked, showing off buff and toned bodies. The bearded dudes are adults, and boys are beardless. The women are modestly clothed, but pull their robes to the side. Before the coming-of-Golden-Age realism and the "wet drapery" technique that enabled

Three-headed demon from the Hekatompedon.

Female kore statue with Archaic smile.

sculptors to portray the bodies beneath robes, this was a crude way to lend some motion and to show a little of their figures. The kore statues are almost always holding something: The Greeks believed women shouldn't approach the gods without a gift of some kind. The equestrian statues represent the upper class, those wealthy elites who owned horses and liked to show them off.

▸ *Halfway down the gallery, on the right against the interior wall, is the...*

❸ Pediment of the Old Temple (Archaios Naos) and Kritios Boy

These sculptures once decorated the temple to Athena next to the Hekatompedon. The temple, damaged after the Persian Wars, was used until the new Parthenon was completed. In the center, Athena, dressed in an ankle-length cloak, strides forward, brandishing a snake as she attacks a giant, who sprawls backward onto his bum. The figures were part of a scene depicting the "Gods Versus Giants" battle atop the temple. The pesky Persians invaded Greece several times over a 50-year period (c. 499-449 B.C.). On the plus side, the wars forced Greeks to band together, and Athens emerged as a dominant naval power. Athenians rebuilt the Acropolis as a symbol of rebirth, with the Parthenon as its centerpiece.

Enjoying the statuary in this hall, you can trace the evolution of Greek art from the static Archaic period to the mastery of the body as a living thing, free and full of movement, in the Golden Age. In the Classical style of fifth-century B.C. Greece, the spine moves realistically with the hips. This is nicely illustrated by the nearby Kritios Boy, 10 steps away. Look up at, and then circle, the Kritios Boy as he gracefully seems to step into Greece's Golden Age.

▸ *Continue down the gallery. Near the up escalator, look for a small, well-preserved marble relief.*

❹ Pensive Athena Relief

The goddess, dressed in a helmet and belted *peplos,* rests her forehead thoughtfully on her spear (460 B.C.). Although she was called "pensive," some think she was actually meant to be mourning the deaths of her citizens in the Persian War.

▸ *Backtrack a tad, then veer left past a bank of elevators. Continue past an open gallery with some statuesque women (we'll visit them in a minute). After the second bank of elevators, look for a series of four squarish marble slabs on your left.*

Pensive Athena, dressed for battle.

Nike lifts her leg to adjust her sandal.

❺ Temple of Athena Nike and Nike Adjusting Her Sandal Reliefs

This set of reliefs (c. 410 B.C.) originally decorated the parapet of the Temple of Athena Nike (which stands near the entrance to the Acropolis). Nike figures had a better chance of survival through the ages than other statues, because anti-pagan Christian vandals mistook the winged Nikes for angels. Nearby is a display containing more chunks of the Temple of Athena Nike. You'll see toes gripping rocks, windblown robes, and realistically twisted bodies—exuberant, life-filled carvings signaling Athens' emergence from the Persian War.

▶ *Turn right and go up the long gallery for a...*

❻ Side-Trip to Hellenistic and Roman Art

Before heading upstairs, continue around on this floor to the small stretch of statues from the Hellenistic and Roman period. The head of Alexander the Great, on a square pillar in the center of the gallery, is a rare original, likely sculpted from life (336 B.C.). Alexander's upper lip curls, and his thick hair sprouts from the center of his forehead—immediately identifying this remarkable man. When he died in 323 B.C., this Macedonian had conquered the rest of Greece, and spread Greek culture throughout the Mediterranean world and as far east as India.

Farther back, visit the spooky "magic sphere" that resembles a dirty soccer ball covered with graffiti. It's actually a marble sphere etched with mysterious symbols (Roman, second or third century A.D.).

▶ *Now turn around, retracing your steps, and turn left at the bank of elevators. Around the corner, on their own, as if starring in their own revue on a beautifully lit stage, are the...*

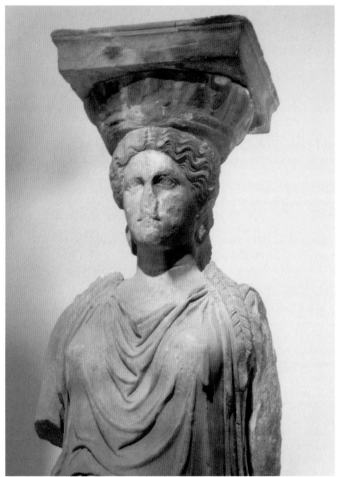

The original Erechtheion Caryatids—ravaged by time and pollution—retain their elegant dignity.

❼ Caryatids from the Erechtheion

Here stand five of the original six lady-columns that once supported the roof of the prestigious Erechtheion temple. (The six on the Acropolis today are copies; another original is in London's British Museum.) Despite their graceful appearance, these sculptures were structurally functional. Each has a fluted column for a leg, a capital-like hat, and buttressing locks of hair in the back. The Caryatids were modeled on and named after the famously upright women of Karyai, near Sparta.

Time and the elements have ravaged these maidens. As recently as the 17th century (see the engravings), they had fragile arms holding ritual bowls for libations. Until the 1950s (before modern smog), their worn-down faces had crisp noses and mouths. In a half-century of Industrial Age pollution, they experienced more destruction than in the previous 2,000 years. But their future looks brighter now that they've been brought indoors out of the acidic air, cleaned up with a laser, and safely preserved for future generations. (For more on the Caryatids in their original location, see page 62.)

There's a glass floor overhead, but you may not want to look up, out of respect for any female visitors wearing dresses above you.

▶ *From the Caryatid gallery, walk to the end of the building. At the relief of Pensive Athena, ride the escalators up. Pause at level 2 to enjoy the view down over the Archaic statues we just visited (the second level has a restaurant and terrace with awesome Acropolis views). Then head for the top floor—it's the reason you're here.*

Level 3

▶ *The escalator deposits you at the "cella"—symbolizing in actual size the inner sanctum of the Parthenon. Before entering the Parthenon Gallery, sit in the atrium and enjoy the video, which covers the temple's 2,500-year history, including a not-so-subtle jab at how Lord Elgin got the marbles and made off with them to England. (For more on Lord Elgin, see page 61.*

Parthenon Models

Two models show how the west and east pediment statues (which are mostly fragments today) would have looked in their prime.

The east pediment (the model on the right) features Nike crowning newly born Athena with a wreath of olive branches. Zeus allowed Athena, the goddess of wisdom, to rise from his brain fully grown and fully armed, to inaugurate the Golden Age of Athens. The other gods at this Olympian banquet—naked men and clothed women—are astounded by the amazing event. At the far left, Helios' four horses are doing their morning chore, dragging the sun out of the sea. And on the far right, Selene, the moon goddess, follows the horses back as she sets into the sea.

The west pediment model (on the left) shows Athena and Poseidon competing for Athens' favor by giving gifts to the city. Poseidon spurts water (beneath him) and Athena presents an olive tree (behind). A big, heavenly audience looks on. Had Poseidon bested Athena, you'd be in Poseidonia today instead of Athens.

▶ Leave this central zone and enter the huge gallery that rings the cella.

The Parthenon Frieze

This top floor re-creates the exact dimensions of the Parthenon—with the frieze (mounted lower for easier viewing), the metopes, and the east and west pediments, all in their proper positions.

Study the museum's highlight—a life-size mock-up of the 525-foot frieze that once wrapped all the way around the outside of the Parthenon. The relief panels depict the Great Panathenaic, the procession held every four years in which citizens climbed up to the Parthenon to celebrate the birth of the city. Circle the perimeter and watch the parade unfold.

Men on horseback, gods, chariots, musicians, priests, riders, officers, warriors, and sacrificial animals are all part of the grand parade, all heading in the same direction—uphill. Prance on. At the heart of the procession are maidens dressed in pleated robes. They shuffle along, carrying gifts for the gods, including incense burners, along with jugs of wine and bowls to pour out offerings. The procession culminates in the presentation of a new *peplos* to Athena, as the gods look on.

Notice the details—for example, the muscles and veins in the horses' legs and the intricate folds in the cloaks and dresses. Some panels have holes drilled in them, where accessories such as gleaming bronze reins were fitted to heighten the festive look. Of course, all of these panels were originally painted in realistic colors. As you move along, notice that, despite the bustle of figures posed every which way, the frieze has one unifying element—most of the people's heads are at the same level, creating a single ribbon around the Parthenon.

Of the original marble frieze, the museum owns only 32 feet. These

Scene from the 525-foot Parthenon frieze, depicting the Panathenaic parade up the Acropolis.

panels were already so acid-worn in 1801 that Lord Elgin didn't bother taking them. Filling in the gaps in this jigsaw puzzle are white plaster replicas of panels still in London's British Museum (marked BM), in Paris' Louvre, and in Copenhagen. Blank spaces represent panels that are forever lost. Small 17th-century engravings show how the frieze looked before the 1687 explosion that devastated the Parthenon.

▶ Now stroll through the gallery and look out the windows. Take a moment to...

Ponder the Parthenon

There's the Parthenon itself, perched on the adjacent hilltop. The Parthenon is one of the most influential works humankind has ever created. For 2,500 years, it's inspired generations of architects, sculptors, painters, engineers, and visitors from around the globe. Here in the Acropolis Museum, you can experience the power of this cultural landmark. The people of Athens relish

The museum's view restaurant—aged wines and the ancient Parthenon.

the Acropolis Museum. Local guides grow taller with every visit, knowing that Greece finally has a suitable place to preserve and share the best of its artistic heritage.

▶ *On your way down, stop by the restaurant on level 2 for its exterior terrace and the awesome view of the Acropolis.*

National Archaeological Museum Tour

ΕΘΝΙΚΟ ΑΡΧΑΙΟΛΟΓΙΚΟ ΜΟΥΣΕΙΟ

The National Archaeological Museum is the top ancient Greek art collection anywhere in the world. Ancient Greece set the tone for all Western art that followed, and this museum lets you trace its evolution, with beautifully displayed and described exhibits from 7000 B.C. to A.D. 500. You'll see the rise and fall of Greece's civilizations: the Minoans, the Mycenaeans, those of Archaic Greece, the Classical Age, and Alexander the Great, and then the Romans. Watch Greek sculpture evolve, from prehistoric Barbie dolls, to stiff Egyptian-style, to the *David*-like balance of the Golden Age, to wet T-shirt, buckin'-bronco Hellenistic, and finally, to the influence of the Romans.

ORIENTATION

Cost: €10, €5 off-season.

Hours: April-Oct daily 8:00-20:00; Nov-March Mon 12:00-17:00, Tue-Sun 8:00-15:00.

Getting There: The museum is a mile north of the Plaka at 28 Oktovriou (a.k.a. Patission) #44. Your best bet is to take a taxi, which costs about €6 from the Plaka. By Metro, use the Omonia stop (as you exit, follow signs to *28 Oktovriou/28 October Street*, and walk seven blocks to the museum—about 15 minutes) or the Victoria stop (about a 10-minute walk). You can also catch a bus to the Polytechneio stop: The #035 leaves from a stop on Athinas street, just north of Monastiraki, and drops you off around the corner from the museum. Bus #224 leaves from Vasilissis Sofias avenue (near Syntagma Square) and stops kitty-corner from the museum.

Information: Tel. 213-214-4800, www.namuseum.gr.

Tours: There are no audioguides, but live guides hang out in the lobby waiting to give you a €50, hour-long tour.

  ⌂ Download my free National Archaeological Museum audio tour.

Length of This Tour: Allow two hours for this tour; more if you want to dig deeper.

Baggage Check: Free and required, except for small purses.

Services: A museum shop, WCs, and an inviting café surround a shady and restful courtyard in the lower level (to access from the main entrance lobby, take the stairs down behind ticket desk); these are easiest to access at the beginning or end of your museum tour.

Photography: Photos are allowed, but no flash and no goofy poses in front of statues. The Greek museum board considers this disrespectful of the ancient culture and is very serious about it.

Starring: The gold Mask of Agamemnon, stately kouros and kore statues, the perfectly posed Artemision Bronze, the horse and jockey of Artemision, and the whole range of Greek art.

THE TOUR BEGINS

The collection is delightfully chronological. To sweep through Greek history, simply visit the numbered rooms in order. From the entrance lobby (Rooms 1-2), start with the rooms directly in front of you (Rooms 3-6), containing prehistoric and Mycenaean artifacts. Then circle clockwise around the building's perimeter on the ground floor (Rooms 7-31) to see the evolution of classical Greek statuary. Keep track of your ticket—you'll need to scan it again to enter some of the exhibits.

This self-guided tour zeroes in on a few choice pieces that give an overview of the collection. Note that my descriptions here are brief—for more detail, read the excellent posted English information in each room.

▸ *From the entrance lobby, go straight ahead into the large central hall (Room 4). This first area—Rooms 3-6—is dedicated to prehistory (7000-1050 B.C.), including the treasures of the Mycenaeans. Start in the small side room to the right, Room 6. In several of this room's cases—including the one directly to the right as you enter—you'll find stiff marble figures with large heads. Look closely into that first case, filled with...*

❶ Cycladic Figurines

Goddess, corpse, fertility figure, good-luck amulet, spirit guide, beloved ancestor, or Neolithic porn? No one knows for sure the purpose of these female figurines, which are older than the Egyptian pyramids. Although these statuettes were made only in the Cycladic Islands, well-traveled ones have been found all over Greece. The earliest Greeks may have worshipped a Great Mother earth goddess long before Zeus and company (variously called Gaia, Ge, and other names), but it's not clear what

Cycladic figures—prehistoric Barbies?

Mask of Agamemnon—a Mycenaean treasure.

National Archaeological Museum

EGYPTIAN ARTIFACTS

41 42 43 44 47

37 36 45 46

40 37A 35

BRONZE STATUES

38 34

39

17 18 14 EPIDAVROS PEDIMENT RELIEFS

16 13 21 22 23 24 15

To Café & WCs

20 19 25 28

3 4 16

CLAY TABLETS WARRIOR KRATER

15 12 FRESCOES 3 6 29 17

14 5 4 26

BASES 10 2 27

13 9

CAFÉ & WCs

10 9 To Café & WCs 19

KOUROI 5 18

11 8 7 2 33 32 31 20

12 8 7 6 ROOM 1 30A

ENTRANCE

VASIL. IRAKLEIOU

N

To M Victoria

CAFÉ

To Plaka & Acropolis

28 OKTOVRIOU (PATISSION)

connection she had, if any, with these statuettes. The ladies are always naked, usually with folded arms. The figures evolved over the years from flat-chested, to violin-shaped, to skinny. There is evidence that the eyes, lips, and ears were originally painted on.

▶ *Return to the long central hall (Room 4), divided into four sections. Here you'll find the...*

❷ Mask of Agamemnon and Other Mycenaean Treasures

Room 4 displays artifacts found in the ruins of the ancient fortress-city of Mycenae, 80 miles west of Athens. You'll see finely decorated swords, daggers, body armor, and jewelry, all found buried alongside bodies in Mycenaean graves. The objects' intricately hammered detail and the elaborate funeral arrangements point to the sophistication of this early culture.

In a glass case in the middle of the second section is the so-called Mask of Agamemnon (c. 1550 B.C.). Made of beaten gold and showing a man's bearded face, this famous mask was tied over the face of a dead man—note the tiny ear-holes for the string.

The Mycenaeans dominated southern Greece a thousand years before the Golden Age (1600-1200 B.C.). Their (real) history was lost in the misty era of Homer's (fanciful) legends of the Trojan War. Then Mycenae was unearthed in the 19th century by the German businessman Heinrich Schliemann (the Indiana Johann of his era). Schliemann, fascinated by the works of Homer, had recently discovered the real-life ruins of Troy (in western Turkey), and he was convinced that Mycenae was the city of the Greeks who'd conquered Troy. That much, at least, may be historically true. Schliemann went on to declare this funeral mask to be that of the legendary King Agamemnon, which *isn't* true, because the mask predates the fall of Troy (c. 1300 B.C.).

▶ *In the next section of Room 4, you'll find...*

❸ More Mycenaean Artifacts

A model of the Acropolis of Mycenae (left side) shows the dramatic hilltop citadel where many of these objects were unearthed. Also in Room 4 are frescoes from the royal palace, done in bright colors in the Minoan style. Clay tablets show the Mycenaean written language known as Linear B, whose syllabic script (in which marks stand for syllables) was cracked only in the 1950s.

At the back side of the display case in the center of this section is a painted, two-handled vase known as the House of the Warrior Krater (#1426)—Schliemann's favorite find. A woman (far left) waves goodbye to a line of warriors heading off to war, with their fancy armor and duffle bags hanging from their spears. Although this provided the world with its first glimpse of a Mycenaean soldier, it's a timeless scene with countless echoes across the generations.

▶ *In the center of the last section of Room 4 is a glass case displaying the...*

❹ Vapheio Cups

These gold cups (c. 1600-1550 B.C.), found with other precious items in a Mycenaean tomb, are metalwork masterpieces. The intricate detail on #1 shows a charging bull sending a guy head over heels. On #2, you'll see a

Warrior Krater shows soldiers off to war.

Vapheio cup—beautiful bovine love.

bull and a cow making eyes at each other, while the hind leg of another bull gets tied up by one good-looking cowboy. These realistic, joyous scenes are the product of the two civilizations that made 15th-century B.C. Greece the wonder of Europe—the Mycenaeans and the Minoan culture of Crete.

Between roughly 1450 and 1150 B.C., the Minoan society collapsed, and Minoan artisans had to find work painting frescoes and making cups for the rising Mycenae culture. Then, around 1100 B.C., the Mycenaeans disappeared from history's radar screen. Whether from invasion, famine, internal strife, or natural disaster, these sudden disappearances plunged Greece into 500 years of Dark Ages (c. 1200-700 B.C.). Little survives from that chaotic time, so let's pick up the thread of history as Greece began to recover a few centuries later.

▶ *Backtrack to the entrance lobby and begin circling clockwise around the perimeter of the building, starting in Room 7. After scanning your ticket again to enter this room, look for the tall vase on your right.*

❺ Dipylon Vase

This monumental ocher-and-black vase (c, 750 B.C.), as tall as a person, is painted with a funeral scene. In the center, the deceased lies on a funeral bier, flanked by a line of mourners, who pull their hair in grief. It's far from realistic. The triangular torsos, square arms, circular heads, and bands of geometric patterns epitomize the style of what's known as the Geometric

The Dipylon vase depicts stick-figure mourners tearing out their hair in grief.

Period (9th-8th century B.C.). A few realistic notes pop through, such as the raw emotions of the mourners and some grazing antelope and ibex (on the neck of the vase).

After four centuries of Dark Ages and war, the Greeks of the eighth century B.C. were finally settling down, establishing cities, and expanding abroad (as seen on the map behind the big vase), with colonies in western Turkey (Ionia), southern Italy (Magna Graecia), and Sicily. They were developing a written language and achieving the social stability that could afford to generate art. This vase is a baby step in that progression. Next, large-scale statues in stone were developed.

▶ *In Rooms 7-14 you'll get a look at some of these giant statues, including the early Greek statues called...*

Kore and Kouros

Some of the earliest surviving examples of post-Mycenaean Greek art (c. 700-480 B.C.) are these life-size and larger-than-life statues of clothed young women (kore/korai) and naked young men (kouros/kouroi). Influenced by ancient statues of Egyptian pharaohs, the earliest of these are big and stiff, with triangular faces and arms at their sides. As you walk through the next few rooms, you'll see the statues become more realistic and natural in their movements, with more personality than we see in these earlier rigid shells.

▶ *Facing the vase in the middle of Room 7 is a...*

❻ Kore, c. 650 B.C.

With hands at her sides, a skinny figure, a rectangular shape, and dressed in a full-length robe (called a chiton), this kore looks as much like a plank of wood as a woman. Her triangular lion-mane hairstyle resembles an Egyptian headdress. The writing down her left leg says she's dedicated to Apollo. Stroll around. The Egyptian influence is clear.

▶ *In the next room (Room 8), your eyes go right to a very nice pair of knees that belong to a...*

❼ Kouros from Sounion, c. 600 B.C.

A typical kouros from the Archaic period (c. 700-480 B.C.), this young naked man has braided dreadlocks and a stable forward-facing pose, and is stepping forward slightly with his left leg. His fists are clenched at his sides, and his scarred face obscures an Archaic smile—a placid smile that suggests the inner secret of happiness. His anatomy is strongly geometrical

Left to right: female statue #1, kouros from Sounion, kore with flower, kouros stepping out.

and stylized, with almond-shaped eyes, oval pecs, an arched rib cage, cylindrical thighs, and a too-perfect symmetry. While less plank-like than earlier statues, he's still much flatter than an actual person. The overdeveloped muscles (look at those quads!) and his narrow waist resemble those of an athletic teenager.

Rather than strict realism, kouros statues capture a geometric ideal. The proportions of the body parts follow strict rules—for example, most later kouros statues are precisely seven "heads" tall. Although this kouros steps forward slightly, his hips remain even (think about it—the hips of a real person would shift forward on one side). The Greeks were obsessed with the human body—remember, these statues were of (idealized) humans, not gods. Standing naked and alone, these statues represented a microcosm of the rational order of nature.

Statues were painted in vivid, lifelike colors. Notice that the rough surface of the marble lacks the translucent sheen of Classical Age statues.

The Four Stages of Greek Sculpture

Archaic (c. 700-480 B.C.): Rigid statues with stylized anatomy, facing forward, with braided hair and mysterious smiles (previous page, far right photo).

Severe (c. 480-460 B.C.): More realistic and balanced statues (with no smiles), capturing a serious nobility. Works from this transitional period are sometimes described as Early Classical.

Classical (c. 460-323 B.C.): Realistic statues of idealized beauty with poses that strike a balance between movement and stillness, with understated emotion. (Within this period, the Golden Age was roughly 450-400 B.C.)

Hellenistic (c. 323-30 B.C.): Photorealistic (even ugly) humans engaged in dramatic, emotional struggles, captured in snapshot poses that can be wildly unbalanced.

(Archaic chisels were not yet strong or efficient enough to avoid shattering the crystalline marble.)

Kouros statues were everywhere, presented as gifts to a god at a sanctuary or to honor the dead in a cemetery. This one was dedicated to Poseidon at the entrance to the temple at Sounion. As a funeral figure, a kouros symbolized the deceased in his prime of youth and happiness, forever young.

▶ *Continue into the next room (Room 11). On the left, holding a flower, is a...*

❽ Kore, c. 550 B.C.

Where a male kouros was naked and either life-size or larger than life (emphasizing masculine power), a female kore was often slightly smaller than life and modestly clothed, capturing feminine grace (males were commonly naked in public, but women never were). This petite kore stands with feet together, wearing a pleated chiton belted at the waist. Her hair is braided and held in place with a diadem (a wreath-like headdress), and she wears a necklace. Her right hand tugs at her dress, indicating motion (a nice trick if the artist lacks the skill to actually show it), while her left hand holds a flower. Like most ancient statues, she was painted in lifelike colors, including her skin. Her dress was red—you can still see traces of the paint—adorned with flower designs and a band of swastikas down the front. (In ancient times—before German archaeologist Schliemann's writings popularized it and Hitler appropriated it—the swastika was a harmless good-luck symbol representing the rays of the sun.) This kore, like all the statues in the room, has that distinct Archaic smile (or smirk, as the Greeks describe it).

▶ *The next room—a long hall labeled Room 13—has...*

❾ More Kouroi and Bases for Funerary Kouroi

These statues, from the late Archaic period (around 500 B.C.), once decorated the tombs of hero athletes—perhaps famous Olympians. Notice that these young men are slightly more relaxed and realistic, with better-formed thighs and bent elbows. Some kouros statues stood on pedestals, like the two square marble bases located farther down Room 13 (left side). The indentations atop each base held a kouros statue that represented an idealized version of the deceased. On the first base, the carved relief shows wrestlers and other athletes. Perhaps this was an excuse for the artist to show off a new ability to depict the body in a twisting pose. Notice the cute dog-and-cat fight. The second base features a field hockey-like game, each scene reflecting the vigor of the deceased man in his prime.

During the Archaic period, Greece was prospering, growing, expanding, trading, and colonizing the Mediterranean. The smiles on the statues capture the bliss of a people settling down and living at peace. But in 480 B.C., Persia invaded, and those smiles soon vanished.

▶ *Pass through Room 14 and into Room 15, which is dominated by one of the jewels of the collection, the...*

❿ Artemision Bronze

This statue was discovered amid a shipwreck off Cape Artemision (north of Athens) in 1928. The weapon was never found, so no one knows for sure if this is Zeus or Poseidon. The god steps forward, raises his arm, sights along his other arm at the distant target, and prepares (if it's Zeus) to hurl his thunderbolt or (if Poseidon) his trident.

The god stands 6'10" and has a physique like mine. His hair is curly and tied at the back, and his now-hollow eyes once shone white with inset bone. He plants his left foot and pushes off with the right. Even though every limb moves in a different direction, the whole effect is one of balance. The statue's dimensions are a study in Greek geometry. His head

The 6'10" bronze god is frozen at the exact moment he's set to hurl his weapon.

is one Greek foot high, and he's six heads tall (or one Greek fathom). The whole figure has an "X" shape that would fit into a perfect circle, with his navel at the center and his fingertips touching the rim. Although the bronze statue—cast with the "lost wax" technique (explained on page 113)—is fully three-dimensional, it's most impressive from the front. (Later Greek statues, from the Hellenistic era, seem fully alive from every angle, including the three-quarter view.)

This Zeus/Poseidon, from c. 460 b.c., is an example of the transition into the Classical style, as sculpture evolved beyond the so-called Severe style (480-460 b.c.). Historically, the Severe/Early Classical Period covers the time when Greece battled the Persians and emerged victorious—the era when ordinary men had also just shaken off tyrants and taken control of their own destiny through democracy. The Greeks were entering the dawn of the Golden Age. During this time of horrific war, the Greeks made art that was serious (no more Archaic smiles), unadorned, and expressed the noble strength and heroism of the individuals who had carried them through tough times. The statues are anatomically realistic, celebrating the human form.

With his movements frozen, as if Zeus/Poseidon were posing for a painting, we can examine the wonder of the physical body. He's natural yet ideal, twisting yet balanced, moving while at rest. With his geometrical perfection and godlike air, the figure sums up all that is best about the art of the ancient world.

Next, we enter the Golden Age. Room 16 is filled with big, tall vases made of marble, labeled ⑪ *Attic Funerary Monuments.* These grave markers take the shape of the ceramic urns used for the ashes of cremated bodies in ancient times. One of these vases (#4485) is particularly touching: A grieving family looks on as Hermes (with his winged sandals) leads a young woman to the underworld.

▶ *Continue through Room 16 and into Room 17. The WCs and café are out the door and downstairs, in the courtyard. From Room 17, turn right into Rooms 19 and 20 (then right again, then left). At the dead end is a small glass case containing the...*

⑫ *Athena Varvakeion*

This marble statue, known as the *Athena Varvakeion* (c. a.d. 250), is considered the most faithful copy of the great *Athena Parthenos* (438 b.c.) by Pheidias. It's essentially a one-twelfth-size replica of the 40-foot statue that once stood in the Parthenon. Although a miniature copy of the glorious original, it provides a good look at Greek art at its Golden Age pinnacle. Athena stands dressed in flowing robes, holding a small figure of Nike (goddess of victory) in her right hand and a shield in her left. Athena's helmet sprouts plumes with winged horses and a sphinx. To give a sense of scale of the original, the tiny Nike in Athena's hand was six feet tall in the Parthenon statue. Athena's covered in snakes. She wears a snake belt and bracelet; coiled snakes decorate her breastplate and one is curled up inside her shield, representing the goddess' connection to her half-snake son, who was born out of the earth and considered to be one of the ancestors of the Athenians. The snake-headed Medusa (whom Athena helped Perseus slay) adorns the center of her chest. (For more on the statue's original location, see my Acropolis Tour, available ⊙ as a chapter in this book and 🎧 as a free audio tour.)

▶ *Backtrack to Room 17, turn right, and continue circling the museum clockwise into Room 18, which has....*

⑬ Funeral Steles

The tombstones that fill this room, all from the fifth century B.C., are more good examples of Golden Age Greek art. With a mastery of the body, artists show poignant scenes of farewell, as loved ones bid a sad goodbye to the dead, who are seated. While the dead are often just shaking hands, there's usually a personal meaning with each scene. For example, on the tombstone on the left wall, a woman who died in childbirth looks at her baby, held by a servant as it reaches for its dead mother. Other scenes include a beautiful young woman, who died in her prime, narcissistically gazing into a mirror. Servants are shown taking part in the sad event, as if considered part of the family. In the center of the room, a rich and powerful

Small-scale version of 40-foot Athena.

Funeral stele—a mother mourns her baby.

woman ponders which treasure from her jewel box to take with her into eternity. Though shallow reliefs, these works are effectively three-dimensional. There's a timeless melancholy in the room, a sense that no matter who you are—or how powerful or affluent your family is—when you go, you go alone...and shrouds have no pockets.

▶ *Pass into Room 21, a large central hall. We'll take a temporary break from the chronological sequence to see statues dating from the second century B.C., when Greece was ruled by Rome. The hall is dominated by the...*

⑭ Artemision Jockey

In this bronze statue (c. 140 B.C.), the horse is in full stride, and the young jockey looks over his shoulder to see if anyone's gaining on them. The statue was recovered in pieces from the seafloor off Cape Artemision. Missing were the reins the jockey once held in his left hand and the whip he used with his right to spur the horse to go even faster—maybe too fast, judging by the look on his face.

Greeks loved their horse races, and this statue may celebrate a victory at one of the Panhellenic Games. The jockey is dressed in a traditional short tunic, has inlaid eyes, and his features indicate that he was probably ethnically part Ethiopian.

The statue, like other ancient bronzes created by Greeks in Roman times, was made not by hammering sheets of metal, but with the classic "lost wax" technique. The artist would first make a rough version of the statue from clay, cover it with a layer of wax, and then cover that with another layer of clay to make a form-fitting mold. When heated in a furnace to harden the mold, the wax would melt—or be "lost"—leaving a narrow space between the clay model and the mold. The artist would then pour molten bronze into the space, let it cool, break the mold, and—*voilà!*—end up with a hollow bronze statue. This particular statue was cast in pieces, which were then welded together. After the cast was removed, the artist added a few surface details and polished it smooth. Notice the delightful detail on the rider's spurs, which were lashed to his bare feet.

Stylistically, we've gone from stiff Archaic, to restrained Severe, to balanced Classical...to this wonderful example of the unbridled emotion of Hellenism.

The other statues in the room are second-century B.C. Roman copies of fifth-century B.C. Greek originals. The Romans were great warriors,

Horse and jockey—unbridled emotion.

Realistic grave relief.

engineers, and administrators, but they had an inferiority complex when it came to art and high culture. For high-class Romans, Greek culture was the ideal, which created a huge demand for Greek statues. As demand exceeded supply, making copies of Greek originals became a big industry, and the Romans excelled at it. In fact, throughout Europe today, when you see a "Greek" statue, it's likely a Roman copy of a Greek original. Thanks to excellent copies like the ones in this room, we know what many (otherwise lost) Golden Age Greek masterpieces looked like.

▶ *To return to our chronological tour (picking up back before the Romans arrived), head into Room 22, with pediment reliefs (Sack of Troy on the right, Greeks vs. Amazons on the left) that once decorated the Temple of Asklepios at Epidavros. Pass through a couple of rooms displaying funeral monuments with progressively higher relief and more monumental scale until you reach the long Room 28, where you'll come face-to-face with a large...*

⑮ Grave Relief of a Horse

The spirited horse steps lively and whinnies while an Ethiopian boy struggles with the bridle and tries to calm him with food. The realistic detail of the horse's muscles and veins is astonishing, offset by the panther-skin blanket. The horse's head pops out of the relief, becoming fully three-dimensional. The boy's pose is slightly off-balance, anticipating the "unposed poses" of later Hellenism (this relief is from the late fourth century B.C.). We sense the emotions of both the overmatched boy and the nervous horse. We also see a balance between the horse and boy, with the two figures creating a natural scene together rather than standing alone.

Bronze youth—perfectly balanced grace.

Philosopher, a Hellenist individual.

▶ *Farther down Room 28 stands the impressive, slightly-larger-than-life-size...*

⑯ Bronze Statue of a Youth

Scholars can't decide whether this statue (c. 340-330 B.C.) is reaching out to give someone an apple or demonstrating a split-finger fastball. He may be Perseus, holding up the head of Medusa, but he's most likely the mythical Paris, awarding a golden apple to the winner of a beauty contest between goddesses (sparking jealousies that started the Trojan War).

The figure is caught in midstep as he reaches out, gazing intently at the person he's giving the object to. Split this youth vertically down the middle to see the *contrapposto* (or "counter-poise") stance of so many Classical statues. His left foot is stable, while the right moves slightly, causing his hips to shift. Meanwhile, his right arm is tense while the left hangs loose. These subtle, contrary motions are in perfect balance around the statue's vertical axis.

In the Classical Age, statues reached their peak of natural realism and balanced grace. During the following Hellenistic Period, sculptors added to that realism, injecting motion and drama. Statues are fully three-dimensional (and Hellenistic statues even more so, as they have no "front": You have to walk around them to see the whole picture). Their poses are less rigid than those in the Archaic period and less overtly heroic than those of the Severe. The beauty of the face, the perfection of the muscles, the balance of elegant grace and brute power—these represent the full ripeness of the art of this age.

▶ *Continue into the small Room 29. To the left of the following door, find a black bronze head in a glass case. Look into the wild and cynical inlaid eyes of this...*

⑰ Head from a Statue of a Philosopher

This philosopher was a Cynic, part of a movement of non-materialist nonconformists founded in the fourth century B.C. by Diogenes. The term "cynic" aptly describes these dislikable, arrogant guys with unkempt hair. The statue's aged, bearded face captures the personality of a distinct individual and is considered a portrait likeness. From c. 240 B.C., it's typical of the Hellenistic Period, the time after the Macedonian Alexander the Great conquered the rest of Greece and proceeded to spread Greek values across much of the Mediterranean and beyond. Hellenistic Greek society promoted a Me-Generation individualism, and artists celebrated everyday people like this. For the first time in history, we see human beings in all their gritty human glory: with wrinkles, male-pattern baldness, saggy boobs, and middle-age spread, all captured in less-than-noble poses.

The glass case to the left shows other parts of his body. The statue was likely shipped in pieces (like an Ikea self-assembly kit) for practical purposes.

This statue, like a number of the museum's statues, was found by archaeologists on the seabed off the coast of Greece. Two separate shipwrecks in ancient times have yielded treasures now in this museum: At the wreck off Cape Artemision, Zeus/Poseidon and the bronze horse and jockey were found. Another wreck, off the tiny island of Antikythira (near the southern tip of the Peloponnesian Peninsula), is the source of this statue, as well as the bronze statue of a youth (the one that's either Paris or Perseus).

▶ *Continue into the long Room 30 and head to the far end to find the...*

⑱ Statue of a Fighting Gaul

Having been wounded in the thigh (note the hole), this soldier has fallen to one knee and reaches up to fend off the next blow. The style of his helmet indicates that he's not a Greek, but a Gaul (from ancient France). The artist catches the exact moment when the tide of battle is about to turn. The face of this Fighting Gaul says he's afraid he may become the Dying Gaul.

The statue (c. 100 B.C.) sums up many of the features of Hellenistic art: He's frozen in motion, in a wild, unbalanced pose that dramatizes his inner thoughts. The diagonal pose runs up his left leg and out his head

Fighting Gaul with unbalanced pose.

Aphrodite, Pan, and Eros flirting.

and outstretched arm. Rather than a noble, idealized god, this is an ordinary soldier caught in an extreme moment. His arms flail, his muscles strain, his eyes bulge, and he cries out in pain. This statue may have been paired with others, creating a theatrical mini-drama that heightened emotion. Hellenism shows us the thrill of victory, and—in this case—the agony of defeat.

▶ *To the right, on the other side of a doorway, is a...*

⑲ Statue of Aphrodite, Pan, and Eros

In this playful marble ensemble (c. 100 B.C.) from the sacred island of Delos, Aphrodite is about to whack Pan with her sandal. Striking a classic *contrapposto* pose (with most of her weight on one foot), Aphrodite is more revealing than modest, her voluptuous body polished smooth. There's a bit of whimsy here, as Aphrodite seems to be saying: "Don't! Stop!"...but may instead be saying: "Don't stop." The actions of the (literally) horny Pan can also be interpreted in two ways: His left arm is forceful, but his right is gentle—holding her more like a dance partner. Eros, like an omnipresent Tinkerbell, comes to Aphrodite's aid—or does he? He has the power to save her if she wants help, but with a hand on Pan's horn and a wink, Eros seems to say: "OK, Pan, this is your chance. Come on, man, go for it." Pan can't believe his luck. This marble is finer than those used in earlier statues, and it has been polished to a sheen with an emery stone. As you walk around this delightful statue, enjoy the detail, from the pudgy baby feet and the remnants of red paint on the sandal to the way the figures all work together in a cohesive vignette.

▶ *Enter Room 31.*

⑳ Statue of the Emperor Augustus

This statue of Augustus, founder of the Roman Empire and its first emperor (c. 12-10 B.C.), is the only known statue of him on horseback, although it is missing its lower half. He holds the (missing) reins in his left hand and raises his right hand in a gesture of blessing or of oration—an expression of the emperor's power. Although Greece was conquered by the Romans (146 B.C.), Greek culture ultimately "conquered" the Romans, as the Grecophile Romans imported Greek statues to Italy to beautify their villas. They preserved Greece's monuments and cranked out high-quality copies of Greek art. When the Roman Emperor Augustus began remaking the city of Rome, he used Greek-style Corinthian columns—a veneer of sophistication on buildings erected with no-nonsense, brick-and-concrete Roman-arch engineering. It's largely thanks to the Romans and their respect for Greek culture that so much of this ancient art survives today.

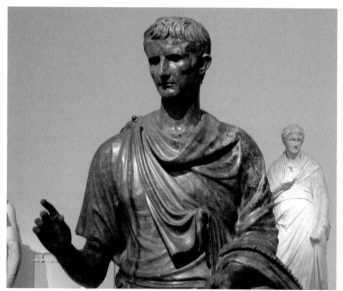

Emperor Augustus and the Romans conquered Greece, but they succumbed to Greek culture.

Sights

Compared to Europe's other big cities, Athens is relatively light on things to do and see. But the few major sights it does have are big-time. The biggies—the Acropolis, Ancient Agora, Acropolis Museum, and National Archaeological Museum—are described in detail in their individual chapters. There you'll find self-guided tours, plus tips on how to avoid lines, save money, and get a decent bite to eat nearby. Other attractions, including churches and less-prominent ancient sights, are also covered in greater depth in my Athens City Walk. If there's more information on a sight elsewhere, it's marked with a ♻.

Be aware that open hours at some sights may vary from those printed in this book. Check locally before planning your day.

To Thissio,
Benaki Museum
of Islamic Art &
Apostolou Pavlou
Pedestrian Zone

Monastiraki   ERMOU

To Central Market,
Omonia Square &
National Archaeological
Museum

ATHINAIDOS

Agia Irini
Square

CHURCH OF
KAPNIKAREA

NORMANOU

Monastiraki
Square

IFESTOU

"SOUVLAKI
ROW"

MONASTIRAKI

AGORA
ENTRANCE

FLEA MARKET

ADRIANOU

Mona-
stiraki

FORMER MOSQUE/
CERAMICS COLLECTION

KAP

PANDROSSOU

ANCIENT
AGORA

MUSEUM OF
GREEK FOLK ART
(2017)

AREOS

LIBRARY
OF HADRIAN

AIOLOU

Cathedral
Square

KLADOU

DEXIPPOU

Agora
Square

AGORA
MUSEUM

PIKILIS

PANOS

FELOPIDA

MUSEUM OF GREEK
POPULAR
INSTRUMENTS

DIOGENOUS

ADRIANOU

POLYGNOTOU

ROMAN
FORUM

TOWER
OF THE
WINDS

KYRRISTOU

ERETHEOS

100 Meters

100 Yards

PANOS

MITROOU

THRASY.

KLEPSYDRAS

LISSIOU

FLESSA

THOLOU

"RESTAURANT
STEPS"

TRIFODON

Mars
Hill

PRYTANIOU

META-
MORPHOSIS

ERECHTHEION

ANAFIOTIKA

AG.
GEORGIOS

THEORIAS

PROPYLAEA

BEULÉ
GATE

ACROPOLIS
TICKETS

ACROPOLIS

STRATONOS

RANGAVA

PARTHENON

OLD ACROPOLIS
MUSEUM

THESPIDOS

ACROPOLIS
ENTRANCE

TEMPLE OF
ATHENA NIKE

EPIMENIDOU

THRASYLLOU

ODEON OF
HERODES ATTICUS

YAKHOU

To Thissio &
Apostolou Pavlou
Pedestrian Zone
"Acropolis Loop"

DIONYSIOU
AREOPAGITOU

"ACROPOLIS LOOP"

THEATER OF
DIONYSUS

Filopappos
Hill

GARIVALDI

ROVERTOU
GALLI

KALLISPERI

MITSEON

ACROPOLIS
MUSEUM

Akropoli

Akropoli

PERIKLEOUS

LEKKA

VOULIS

KARA. SERV.

SYNTAGMA

HOTEL GRANDE
BRETAGNE

Syntagma

VAS. SOFIAS

VAS. GEORGIOU

To Benaki Museum,
Museum of Cycladic Art,
National War Museum,
Byzantine and
Christian Museum
& Lykavittos Hill

FOKIONOS

SKOPA

ERMOU

Bus #X80
to / from Piraeus

Syntagma
Square

CATHEDRAL
(MITROPOLIS)

PETRAKI

IPATIAS

MITROPOLEOS

POST

PARLIAMENT

Syntagma

CHURCH OF AGIOS
ELEFTHERIOS

OTHONOS

TOMB OF
THE UNKNOWN
SOLDIER

APOLLONOS

IPITOU

SKOUFOU

VOULIS

NIKIS

FILELLINON

Bus #X95
to Airport

Syntagma

AG. FILOTHEIS

XENOFONDOS

AG.
FILOTHEIS

NIKODIMOU

PLAKA

IPERIDOU

JEWISH
MUSEUM
OF GREECE

Y. SOURI

PSYLLA

Bus #040
from Piraeus

National
Garden

THOLOU

ADRIANOU

SOTIROU

CINE PARIS
(OUTDOOR
MOVIES)

KIDATHINEON

Filomousou
Square

DEDALOU

SHELLY

AG.
AIKATERINI

THOLOU

PITTAKOU

GOURA

ZAPPEION
(EXHIBITION HALL)

LYSICRATES
MONUMENT

LYSIKRATOUS

FEKYNIHOU

SONOXKIA

ARCH OF
HADRIAN

Bus #X80
from Piraeus

TEMPLE OF
OLYMPIAN ZEUS

MAKRI

TZIREON

Bus #X80
to Piraeus

VASILISSIS AMALIAS

VASILISSIS OLGAS

To
Panathenaic
Stadium

ACROPOLIS AND NEARBY

A broad pedestrian boulevard that I call the "Acropolis Loop" strings together the Acropolis, Mars Hill, Theater of Dionysus, Acropolis Museum, and the Ancient Agora.

▲▲▲Acropolis

The most important ancient site in the Western world, the Acropolis (which means "high city" in Greek) rises gleaming like a beacon above the gray concrete drudgery of modern Athens. This is where the Greeks built the mighty Parthenon—the most famous temple on the planet and an enduring symbol of ancient Athens' glorious Golden Age from nearly 2,500 years ago.

> ✪ See the Acropolis Tour chapter.

▲▲"Acropolis Loop"

One of Athens' best attractions, this wide, well-manicured, delightfully traffic-free pedestrian boulevard borders the Acropolis to the south and east. It's composed of two streets with tongue-twisting names—Dionysiou Areopagitou and Apostolou Pavlou (think of them as Dionysus Street and Apostle Paul's Street); for simplicity, I refer to them collectively as the "Acropolis Loop." One of the city's many big improvements made in preparation for its 2004 Olympics-hosting bid, this walkway immediately became a favorite local hangout, with vendors, al fresco cafés, and frequent special events enlivening its cobbles.

Dionysiou Areopagitou, wide and touristy, runs along the southern base of the Acropolis. It was named for Dionysus the Areopagite, first bishop and patron saint of Athens and a member of the ancient Roman-era senate that met atop Mars Hill (described next). The other section, **Apostolou Pavlou**—quieter, narrower, and tree-lined—curls around the western end of the Acropolis and the Ancient Agora. It feels more local and has the best concentration of outdoor eateries (in the Thissio neighborhood). This section was named for the Apostle Paul, who presented himself before Dionysus the Areopagite at Mars Hill.

▲Mars Hill (Areopagus)

The knobby, windswept hill crawling with tourists in front of the Acropolis is Mars Hill, also known as Areopagus (from *Areios Pagos,* "Ares Hill,"

Acropolis Tickets

A basic Acropolis ticket costs €20 (€10 Nov-March) and covers entry to the Acropolis, as well as access to sights on the north and south slopes, including the Theater of Dionysus. If you plan to visit Athens' other major ancient sites, the €30 Acropolis combo-ticket is the better deal, as it covers not only the Acropolis and Theater of Dionysus, but also the Ancient Agora (€8), Roman Forum (€6), Temple of Olympian Zeus (€6), Library of Hadrian (€4), and Keramikos Cemetery (€8; individual entry prices are cut in half for all of these sights in winter; no winter discount on combo-ticket). The combo-ticket is valid for five days, and since you can buy it at any participating sight, it allows you to skip the ticket-buying line at the Acropolis. The Acropolis-only ticket must be purchased at the Acropolis ticket office.

Note that these sights are always free for those 18 and under. They're also free on national holidays and on the first Sunday of the month from November through March.

referring to the Greek version of Mars). While the views from the Acropolis are more striking, rugged Mars Hill (near the Acropolis' main entrance, at the western end) makes a pleasant perch. As you're climbing Mars Hill, be warned: The stone stairs (and the top of the rock) have been polished to a slippery shine by history, and can be treacherous even when dry. Watch your step and use the metal staircase.

This hill has an interesting history. After Rome conquered Athens in 86 B.C., the Roman overlords wisely decided to extend citizenship to any free man born here. (The feisty Greeks were less likely to rise up against a state that had made them citizens.) Whereas Rome called the shots on major issues, minor matters of local governance were determined on this hill by a gathering of leaders. During this time, the Apostle Paul—the first great Christian missionary and author of about half of the New Testament—preached to the Athenians here on Mars Hill. Paul looked out over the Agora and started talking about an altar he'd seen—presumably in the Agora (though archaeologists can't confirm)—to the "Unknown God." (A plaque embedded in the rock near the stairs contains the Greek text of Paul's speech.) Although the Athenians were famously open-minded, Paul encountered a skeptical audience and only netted a couple of converts (including Dionysus the Areopagite—the namesake of the pedestrian drag behind the Acropolis). Paul moved on to Corinth where he enjoyed a better reception.

Theater of Dionysus

The scant remains of this theater are scattered southeast of the Acropolis, just above the Dionysiou Areopagitou walkway. During Roman times, the theater was connected to the Odeon of Herodes Atticus (see page 48) by a long, covered stoa, creating an ensemble of inviting venues. But its illustrious history dates back well before that: It's fair to say that this is where our culture's great tradition of theater was born. During Athens' Golden Age, Sophocles and others watched their plays performed here. Originally just grass, with a circular dirt area as the stage, the theater was eventually expanded, and stone seating added, to accommodate 17,000 patrons in about 330 B.C., during the time of Alexander the Great. Later the Romans added a raised stage. Because the theater is included in your Acropolis ticket, consider a stroll through its rubble. Plans are afoot to restore the theater to its former greatness.

▸ *Covered by €20 Acropolis ticket and €30 Acropolis combo-ticket, same hours as Acropolis, main gate across from Acropolis Museum, tel. 210-322-4625.*

▲▲▲Acropolis Museum

Located at the foot of Athens' famous ancient hill, this modern-day temple to the Acropolis contains relics from Greece's most famous sight.

✪ See the Acropolis Museum Tour chapter.

ANCIENT AGORA AND BEYOND

▲▲▲Ancient Agora: Athens' Market

Although literally and figuratively overshadowed by the impressive Acropolis, the Agora was for eight centuries the true meeting place of the city—a hive of commerce, politics, and everyday bustle.

✪ See the Ancient Agora Tour chapter.

▲▲Thissio and Psyrri

These two neighborhoods, just west and north (respectively) of the Ancient Agora, offer a real-world alternative to the tourist-clogged, artificial-feeling Plaka. Thissio, around the far side of the Acropolis (just follow the main pedestrian drag) has a trendy, yuppie vibe and a thriving passel of cafés and restaurants with Acropolis views. Psyrri—the yang to Thissio's yin—is grungy and run-down, but increasingly populated by a wide range of eateries, cafés, and clubs, with everything from dives to exclusive dance halls to crank-'em-out chain restaurants. While enjoyable at any time of day, both neighborhoods are ideal in the evening—either for dinner or for a stroll afterward.

Benaki Museum of Islamic Art

Sometimes it seems the Greeks would rather just forget the Ottoman chapter of their past...but when you're talking about nearly 400 years, that's difficult to do. If you're intrigued by what Greeks consider a low point in their history, pay a visit to this branch of the prominent, private Benaki Museum (see listing for main branch on page 131). The 8,000-piece

Great nightlife and views in Thissio.

collection, displayed in two renovated Neoclassical buildings, includes beautifully painted ceramics, a rare 14th-century astrolabe, and an entire marble room from a 17th-century Cairo mansion.

▶ *€7, Thu-Sun 9:00-17:00, closed Mon-Wed, Agion Asomaton 22, on the corner with Dipilou, Metro: Thissio, tel. 210-325-1311, www.benaki.gr.*

IN SYNTAGMA

These three sights are covered in more detail in the Athens City Walk ☺ chapter and 🎧 audio tour.

▲Syntagma Square (Plateia Syntagmatos)

The "Times Square" of Athens is named for Greece's historic 1843 constitution, prompted by demonstrations right on this square. A major transit hub, the square is watched over by Neoclassical masterpieces such as the Hotel Grande Bretagne and the Parliament building.

Parliament

The former palace of King Otto is now a house of democracy. In front, colorfully costumed evzone guards stand at attention at the Tomb of the Unknown Soldier and periodically do a ceremonial changing of the guard to the delight of tourists (guards change five minutes before the top of each hour, less elaborate crossing of the guard around :25 after, full ceremony with marching band most Sundays at 11:00—get there early as they may start a bit before 11:00).

Ermou Street

This pedestrianized thoroughfare, connecting Syntagma Square with Monastiraki (and on to Thissio), is packed with top-quality international shops. While most Athenians can't afford to shop here, it's enjoyable for people-watching and is refreshingly traffic-free in an otherwise congested area.

CHURCHES IN THE PLAKA

All of these sights are covered in detail in the Athens City Walk ⚙ chapter and 🎧 audio tour. Only the basics are listed here.

▲Church of Kapnikarea

Sitting unassumingly in the middle of Ermou street, this small, 11th-century Byzantine church offers a convenient look at the Greek Orthodox faith.

▸ *Free, likely open daily 8:30-13:30 plus Tue and Thu-Fri 17:00-19:30.*

Cathedral (Mitropolis)

Dating from the mid-19th century, this big but stark head church of Athens—and therefore of all of Greece—is covered in scaffolding. The cathedral is the centerpiece of a reverent neighborhood, with a pair of statues out front honoring great heroes of the Church, surrounding streets lined with religious paraphernalia shops (and black-cloaked, long-bearded priests), and the cute little Church of Agios Eleftherios (described next).

▸ *Free, generally open daily 8:00-13:00 & 16:30-19:00, no afternoon closure in summer, Plateia Mitropoleos.*

▲Church of Agios Eleftherios

This tiny church, huddled in the shadow of the cathedral, has a delightful hodgepodge of ancient and early Christian monuments embedded in its facade. Like so many Byzantine churches, it was partly built (in the late 12th century) with fragments of earlier buildings, monuments, and even tombstones. Today it's a giant *Da Vinci Code*-style puzzle of millennia-old bits and pieces.

▸ *Free, likely open daily 8:30-13:30 & 17:00-19:30, Plateia Mitropoleos.*

EAST OF THE PLAKA

These two sights, dating from Athens' Roman period, overlook a busy highway at the edge of the tourist zone (just a few steps up Dionysiou Areopagitou from the Acropolis Museum and Akropoli Metro stop, or a 10-minute walk south of Syntagma Square). Both are described in greater detail in the Athens City Walk ⚙ chapter and 🎧 audio tour.

Sights

▲Arch of Hadrian

This stoic triumphal arch stands at the edge of the new suburb of ancient Athens built by the Roman Emperor Hadrian in the second century A.D.

▶ *Always viewable.*

▲▲Temple of Olympian Zeus

Started by an overambitious tyrant in the sixth century B.C., this giant temple was not completed until Hadrian took over, seven centuries later. Now 15 of the original 104 Corinthian columns stand evocatively over a ruined base in a field. You can get a good view of the temple ruins through the fence by the Arch of Hadrian, but since the sight is included in the Acropolis ticket, you can easily drop in for a closer look.

▶ *€6, covered by Acropolis combo-ticket, daily May-Sept 8:00-20:00, April and Oct 8:00-19:00, Nov-March 8:00-15:00, Vasilissis Olgas 1, Metro: Akropoli, tel. 210-922-6330, www.culture.gr.*

SOUTH AND EAST OF THE PARLIAMENT AND SYNTAGMA SQUARE

The busy avenue called Vasilissis Amalias rumbles south of Syntagma Square, where you'll find the following sights. Note that the Arch of Hadrian and the Temple of Olympian Zeus (both described earlier) are just south of the National Garden and Zappeion.

National Garden

Extending south from the Parliament, the National Garden is a wonderfully cool retreat from the traffic-clogged streets of central Athens. Covering an area of around 40 acres, it was planted in 1839 as the palace garden, created for the pleasure of Queen Amalia. Opened to the public in 1923, the garden has many pleasant paths, a café, WCs, scattered picturesque ancient columns, a playground, and several zoo-type exhibits of animals.

▶ *Free, open daily from dawn to dusk.*

Zappeion

At the southern end of the National Garden stands the grand mansion called the Zappeion, surrounded by formal gardens of its own. To most Athenians, the Zappeion is best known as the site of the Aigli Village outdoor cinema in summer (behind the building, on the right as you face the colonnaded main entry; for details, see page 171). But the building is more than just a backdrop. During Ottoman rule, much of the Greek elite, intelligentsia, and aristocracy fled the country. They returned after independence and built grand mansions such as this. Finished in 1888, it was designed by the Danish architect Theophilus Hansen, who was known (along with his brother Christian) for his Neoclassical designs. The financing was provided by the Zappas brothers, Evangelos and Konstantinos, two of the prime movers in the campaign to revive the Olympic Games. This mansion housed the International Olympic Committee during the first modern Olympics in 1896 and served as a media center during the 2004 Olympics. Today the Zappeion is a conference and exhibition center.

▶ *Gardens free and always open, building only open during exhibitions for a fee, Vasilissis Amalias, Metro: Akropoli or Evangelismos.*

Sights

▲Panathenaic (a.k.a. "Olympic") Stadium

Here's your chance to see an intact ancient stadium. This gleaming marble stadium has many names. Officially it's the Panathenaic Stadium, built in the fourth century B.C. to host the Panathenaic Games. Sometimes it's referred to as the Roman Stadium, because it was rebuilt by the great Roman benefactor Herodes Atticus in the second century A.D., using the same prized Pentelic marble that was used in the Parthenon. This magnificent white marble gives the place its most popular name: Kalimarmaro ("Beautiful Marble") Stadium. It was restored to its Roman condition in preparation for the first modern Olympics in 1896. It saw Olympic action again in 2004, when it provided a grand finish for the marathon and a wonderful backdrop for the Paralympics opening ceremony. Today, it's

The white-marbled Panathenaic Stadium.

Central Market—where the locals shop.

occasionally used for ceremonies and concerts. In ancient times, around 50,000 spectators filled the stadium; today, 45,000 people can pack the stands.

▶ *€5, includes good audioguide, daily March-Oct 8:00-19:00, Nov-Feb 8:00-17:00, southeast of the Zappeion off Vasileos Konstantinou, Metro: Akropoli or Evangelismos, tel. 210-752-2985, www.panathenaicstadium.gr.*

NORTH OF MONASTIRAKI

Athinas street leads north from Monastiraki Square to Omonia Square. Walking this grand street offers a great chance to feel the pulse of modern, workaday Athens, with shops tumbling onto broad sidewalks, striking squares, nine-to-fivers out having a smoke, and lots of urban energy. Central Market is on the way to Omonia Square. Farther up Athinas street, past Omonia Square, is the National Archaeological Museum.

Central Market

Take a vibrant, fragrant stroll through the modern-day version of the Ancient Agora. It's a living, breathing, and smelly barrage on all the senses. You'll see dripping-fresh meat, livestock in all stages of dismemberment, still-wriggling fish, exotic nuts, and sticky figs. It may not be Europe's most colorful or appealing market, but it offers a lively contrast to Athens' ancient sites.

The entire market square is a delight to explore, with colorful and dirt-cheap souvlaki shops and a carnival of people-watching. The best and cheapest selection of whatever's in season is at the fruit and vegetable stalls, which spread across Athinas street downhill to the west and are flanked by shops selling a dozen different kinds of olives and feta from the barrel. Meat and fish markets are housed in the Neoclassical building to the east, behind a row of shops facing Athinas street that specialize in dried fruit and nuts. Try the roasted almonds and the delicious white figs from the island of Evia. For a memorable drink and snack, seek out the **Karayiannis Ouzo Bar,** in the market's fish section.

▶ *Open Mon-Sat 7:00-15:00, closed Sun, on Athinas between Sofokleous and Evripidou, between Metro stops Omonia and Monastiraki.*

▲▲▲National Archaeological Museum

This museum is the single best place on earth to see ancient Greek artifacts, from 7,000 B.C. to A.D. 500.

　✪ See National Archaeological Museum Tour chapter.

THE KOLONAKI MUSEUM STRIP, EAST OF SYNTAGMA SQUARE

The district called Kolonaki, once the terrain of high-society bigwigs eager to live close to the Royal Palace (now the Parliament), is today's diplomatic quarter. Lining the major boulevard called Vasilissis Sofias are many embassies, a thriving local yuppie scene, and some of Athens' top museums outside the old center. These are listed in the order you'd reach them, heading east from the Parliament.

▲▲Benaki Museum of Greek History and Culture

This exquisite collection takes you on a fascinating walk through the ages. And, as it's housed in a gorgeous Neoclassical mansion, it gives a peek at how Athens' "one percent" lived back in the 19th century. The mind-boggling array of artifacts—which could keep a museum lover busy for hours—is crammed into 36 galleries on four floors, covering seemingly every era of history: antiquity, Byzantine, Ottoman, and modern. The private collection nicely complements the many state-run museums in town. Each item is labeled in English, and it's all air-conditioned. The Benaki gift shop is a fine place to buy jewelry (replicas of museum pieces).

　First you'll see fine painted vases, gold wreaths of myrtle leaves worn on heads 2,300 years ago, and evocative Byzantine icons and jewelry. Look for Byzantine icon art, including two pieces by Domenikos Theotokopoulos before he became El Greco (glass case in center of room). Upstairs, the first floor picks up where most Athens museums leave off: the period of Ottoman and Venetian occupation. Here you'll find traditional costumes, furniture, household items, farm implements, musical instruments, and entire rooms finely carved from wood and lovingly transplanted from Northern Greece. In Rooms 22 and 23, a fascinating exhibit shows Greece through the eyes of foreign visitors, who came here in the 18th and 19th centuries (back when Athens was still a village, spiny with Ottoman minarets) to see the same ruins you're enjoying today. On the top floor,

Sights

Romantic art depicts Greece's stirring and successful 19th-century struggle for independence.

▶ €7, free entry on Thu; open Wed and Fri 9:00-17:00, Thu and Sat 9:00-24:00, Sun 9:00-15:00, closed Mon-Tue; classy rooftop café where some of today's high society hang out, across from back corner of National Garden at Koumbari 1, Metro: Syntagma, tel. 210-367-1000, www.benaki.gr.

▲▲Museum of Cycladic Art

This modern, cozy museum shows off the largest exhibit of Cycladic art anywhere, collected by one of Greece's richest shipping families (the Goulandris clan). While you can see Cycladic art elsewhere in Athens (such as in the National Archaeological Museum), it's displayed and described most invitingly here. While the first floor is all Cycladic, there are four floors—each with a fine exhibit.

The first floor up focuses on art from the Cycladic Islands, which surround the isle of Delos, off the coast southeast of Athens. The Aegean city-states here—predating Athens' Golden Age by 2,000 years—were populated by a mysterious people who left no written record. But they did leave behind an ample collection of fertility figurines. These come in different sizes but follow the same general pattern: skinny, standing ramrod-straight, with large alien-like heads.

While that first floor is the headliner, don't miss three more floors of exhibits upstairs: ancient Greek art, Cypriot antiquities, and scenes from daily life in antiquity. The highlight—for some, even better than the Cycladic art itself—is the engrossing top-floor exhibit that explains ancient Greek lifestyles. Artifacts, engaging illustrations, and vivid English descriptions resurrect a fun cross-section of the fascinating and sometimes bizarre practices of the ancients: weddings, athletics, agora culture, warfare, and various female- and male-only activities (such as the male-bonding/dining ritual called the symposium).

▶ €7, half-price on Mon and off-season; Mon and Wed-Sat 10:00-17:00, Thu until 20:00, Sun 11:00-17:00, closed Tue and many religious holidays; Neophytou Douka 4, Metro: Evangelismos; the museum's entrance is a few steps up the side street (Neophytou Douka), while the more prominent corner building, fronting Vasilissis Sofias, is their larger annex (or "New Wing"), hosting special exhibits; tel. 210-722-8321, www.cycladic.gr.

▲▲Byzantine and Christian Museum

This excellent museum displays key artifacts from the Byzantine Empire, covering the chapters of the Greek story that come after its famed Golden Age. It traces the era from Emperor Constantine's move from Rome to Byzantium (which he renamed Constantinople, now known as Istanbul) in A.D. 330 until the fall of Constantinople to the Ottomans in 1453. While the rest of Europe fell into the Dark Ages, Byzantium shone brightly. And, as its dominant language and education were Greek, today's Greeks proudly consider the Byzantine Empire "theirs." Outside of the Golden Age of antiquity, the Byzantine era is considered the high-water mark for Greek culture.

The permanent exhibit (the building on the left) is organized both chronologically and thematically. It traces the story of the Byzantine Empire, from the waning days of antiquity through the fledgling days of early Christianity and on to the glory days of Byzantium. It's divided into two sections. The first section, "From the Ancient World to Byzantium," explains how the earliest Byzantine Christians borrowed artistic forms from the Greek and Roman past, and adapted them to fit their emerging beliefs. View mosaics and capitals from the earliest "temples" of Christianity and see how existing ancient temples were "Christianized" for new use. The second section, "The Byzantine World," delves into various facets of Byzantium—the administration of a vast empire, the use of art in early Christian worship, wall paintings transplanted from a Byzantine church, the role of Athens (and the surrounding region of Attica) in the Byzantine Empire, the introduction of Western European artistic elements by Frankish and Latin Crusaders during the 13th century, everyday countryside lifestyles (to balance out all that stuffy ecclesiastical art), the final artistic flourishing of the 13th and 14th centuries, and the fall of

The fine Byzantine and Christian Museum.

History and weaponry at the war museum.

Constantinople (and the Byzantine emperor) to Ottoman Sultan Mehmet the Conqueror.

▶ €8, April-Oct daily 8:00-20:00; Nov-March Tue-Sun 9:00-16:00, closed Mon; excellent café/restaurant, Vasilissis Sofias 22, Metro: Evangelismos, tel. 210-213-9501, www.byzantinemuseum.gr.

National War Museum

This imposing three-story museum documents the history of Greek warfare, from Alexander the Great to today. The overtly patriotic exhibit, staffed by members of the armed forces, stirs the Greek soul. Start by riding the elevator upstairs to the first floor. Here you'll get a quick chronological review of Greek military history, including replicas of ancient artifacts you'll see for real in other museums. The mezzanine level focuses on the Greek experience in the 20th century, including World War I (with amazing video clips) and World War II (Nazi occupation, resistance, and liberation). Back on the ground floor, you'll parade past military uniforms, browse an armory of old weapons, and (outside) ogle modern military machines—tanks, fighter jets, and more.

▶ €3, May-Oct Tue-Sat 9:00-19:00, Sun 9:30-17:00, closed Mon, closes two hours earlier off-season, Rizari 2 at Vasilissis Sofias, Metro: Evangelismos, tel. 210-725-2975, www.warmuseum.gr.

DAY TRIPS FROM ATHENS

The following destinations are doable in a day from Athens. But they'll be much more satisfying with an overnight or as part of a longer Greece itinerary. For more information, see my Rick Steves Greece: Athens & the Peloponnese guidebook.

▲▲▲Hydra

In under two hours, you can sail to this glamorous getaway, combining practical convenience with idyllic Greek island ambience. While Hydra (EE-drah) can be done as a long day trip from Athens, it's better to spend two nights (or more) so you can really relax.

One of the island's greatest attractions is its total absence of cars and motorbikes. Sure-footed donkeys—laden with everything from sandbags and bathtubs to bottled water—climb stepped lanes. The island's main

Hydra—Greek-isle ambience two hours away. On Hydra, donkeys do the heavy lifting.

town, also called Hydra, is one of Greece's prettiest. Its busy but quaint harbor—bobbing with rustic fishing boats and luxury yachts—is surrounded by a ring of rocky hills and whitewashed homes. From the harbor, zippy water taxis whisk you to isolated beaches and tavernas.

▶ *Getting There:* *To reach Hydra, take a Hellenic Seaways high-speed hydrofoil ("Flying Dolphin") or catamaran ("Flying Cat"). Boats leave from the port of Piraeus (near central Athens—see page 161) frequently (6-8/ day June-Sept, 4/day Oct-May, 1.5-2 hours; for tickets, visit a travel agency, call, or go online—tel. 210-419-9000, www.hellenicseaways.gr). Note that it's wise to book well in advance, especially for summer weekends, and that weather conditions can cause cancellations.*

▲▲Delphi

Outside of Athens, this is the most spectacular of Greece's ancient sites. Long ago, Delphi (dell-FEE) was the home of a prophetess known as the oracle (a.k.a. the Pythia or sibyl), the mouthpiece of Apollo on earth. Pilgrims came from far and wide to seek her advice on everything from affairs of state to wars to matrimonial problems. Delphi's fame grew, and its religious festivals blossomed into the Pythian Games, an athletic contest that was second only to the Olympics. Today visitors can see the archaeological site, containing the ruins of the Sanctuary of Apollo, and the great Delphi Archaeological Museum, where statues and treasures found on the site help bring the ruins to life.

▶ *€12 to enter both the site and museum (€6 off-season or if visiting only one or the other); 18 and under free—be prepared to show ID; both the site and museum are open daily 8:00-20:00 in summer (generally April-Oct); in winter, both are open daily 8:00-15:00 (generally Nov-March, but*

Delphi's photogenic Sanctuary of Athena.

winter schedule can be extended). Upon your arrival in Delphi, confirm opening times either with your hotel or in person by stopping by the museum or site, tel. 22650-82312, www.culture.gr.

Getting There: *Buses between Delphi and Athens depart every few hours (roughly 5/day, 3 hours). It's a 10-minute walk to the archaeological site from the bus stop (smart to buy return ticket as soon as you arrive, because buses can fill up). Or join a package tour from Athens, which includes transportation, a guided tour, and lunch (see page 171).*

The Peloponnese

The Peloponnese is the large peninsula that hangs from the rest of the Greek mainland by the narrow Isthmus of Corinth. Though you can day-trip to any of these places from Athens, if you have time, it's best to hunker down in Nafplio for two or three nights, using it as a launchpad for your ancient sightseeing.

▲▲▲Nafplio

Once the capital of a newly independent Greece (19th century), this historically important town is as chic as Athens, without all the graffiti. While the town's glory days have faded, Nafplio retains a certain genteel panache.

Walk the narrow and atmospheric back streets, lined with elegant Venetian houses and Neoclassical mansions. Dip into the fine archaeological museum, featuring relics from prehistoric Greece and the Mycenaean civilization. Or hike up to Palamidi Fortress, one of three Venetian-built castles guarding the harbor (all wonderfully floodlit at night). The best-preserved castle of its kind in Greece, Palamidi towers over the Old Town, protected to the west by steep cliffs that plunge 650 feet to the sea.

▶ *Getting There: It's an easy 2.5-hour drive or bus ride from Athens (buses run nearly hourly, www.ktel-argolidas.gr).*

▲Epidavros

Nestled in a leafy valley some 20 miles east of Nafplio, Epidavros was once the most famous healing center in the ancient Greek world. Since pilgrims prayed to Asklepios, the god of medicine, for health, a sanctuary was needed, with a temple, altars, and statues to the gods. The sanctuary reached the height of its popularity in the fourth and third centuries B.C., when it boasted medical facilities, housing for the sick, mineral baths, a stadium for athletic competitions, and a theater. These days the famous theater is Epidavros' star attraction. Built into the side of a tree-covered hill, it's the finest and best-preserved of all of Greece's ancient theaters—and that's saying something in a country with 132 of them.

▶ *€12 (€6 off-season) includes theater, museum, and archaeological site; daily April-Oct 8:00-20:00, off-season 8:00-15:00, check times locally; tel. 27350-22009, www.culture.gr.*

Getting There: From Nafplio, it's a 30-minute drive or bus ride (Mon-Sat 2-3/day). From Athens, buses head to Nafplio, then continue on to

Nafplio—history, atmosphere, and seafood.

Test the acoustics at Epidavros' theater.

Epidavros (2-3/day, 2.5 hours, might require a transfer in Nafplio, www. ktel-argolidas.gr).

▲Mycenae

This fortress city atop a hill was the hub of a mighty civilization that dominated the Greek world between 1600 and 1200 B.C., a thousand years before Athens' Golden Age. Today, a visit to Mycenae is a trip back into prehistory to see some of the oldest remains (in Europe) of a complex civilization. The three main attractions are the archaeological ruins, consisting of the hilltop walled city with its grand Lion Gate entrance; a museum housing artifacts that were found here; and the impressive Treasury of Atreus—a huge domed tomb where Mycenae's royalty were buried.

▶ *€12 (€6 off-season) includes archaeological site, museum, and Treasury of Atreus; roughly May-Oct daily 8:00-20:00, closes an hour or two earlier in fall; Nov-April daily 7:30-15:00 or 8:30-16:00, may close Sun; hours can change without notice—call ahead to confirm; tel. 27510-76802 (at Mycenae) or 27520-27502 (in Nafplio), www.culture.gr.*

Getting There: *It's 45 minutes by car or bus from Nafplio (Mon-Sat 2-3/day, confirm that your bus goes to the archaeological site—other buses take you only as far as Fichti, two miles away; www.ktel-argolidas.gr).*

Mycenae's Treasury of Atreus: royal burial place.

Sights

Sleeping

Greece's economic struggles translate into good values at Athens hotels. Still, small, inexpensive hotels in the Plaka and Syntagma area are relatively scarce, listed in all the guidebooks, and filled with other tourists. Be willing to expand your search beyond the old center. I've found several gems in Makrigianni and Koukaki (behind the Acropolis and a short walk from the Plaka). These typically offer better value and a more sedate and authentic (rather than bustling and touristy) experience. I like hotels that are clean, central, a good value, and friendly, with local character and simple facilities that don't cater to American "needs."

Double rooms listed in this book average about €90, ranging from €55 (very simple, toilet and shower down the hall) to €350 (maximum plumbing and more).

Hotel Price Code

$$$ Most rooms are €100 or more.
$$ Most rooms between €75–100.
$ Most rooms €75 or less.

Unless otherwise noted, breakfast is included, English is spoken, and free Wi-Fi is available. Many places accept credit cards, and rooms generally have air-conditioning. Prices can change; verify current rates online or by email. For the best prices, always book directly with the hotel.

A Typical Athens Hotel

A €90 double room in Athens is small by American standards and has one double bed (either queen-sized or slightly narrower) or two twins. If you want a bathtub, ask about one when you reserve, as most hotel bathrooms have just a shower. Most bathrooms have ancient plumbing that clogs easily. Rather than flushing toilet paper, dispose of it in the wastebasket next to the toilet. Rooms generally have a telephone and TV, and may have a safe. Most hotels at this price will have air-conditioning—cheaper places may not.

In general, lower your expectations. In ramshackle Athens, any room less than €75 will likely be clean, but expect well-worn bathrooms and furnishings.

A satisfying Greek breakfast with cheese, ham, yogurt, fresh bread, honey, jam, fruit, juice, and coffee or tea is standard and is sometimes included in hotel prices.

Hoteliers can be a great help and source of advice. Most know their city well, and can assist you with everything from public transit and airport connections to finding a good restaurant, the nearest launderette, or Wi-Fi hotspot. Most staff speak at least enough English to get by.

Hotels are required by law to be nonsmoking, but enforcement is spotty. Hoteliers are obsessive about cleaning out odors, but if your room smells like the Marlboro man slept there, ask to be moved.

Athens is a noisy city, and Athenians like to stay out late. This, plus heavy street traffic, can challenge light sleepers. I've tried to recommend places in quieter areas, but finding a peaceful corner isn't always possible. Many hotels were renovated for the 2004 Olympics, adding "soundproof" doors and windows that can help block out noise. Still, be ready to use earplugs.

Making Reservations

Make reservations by phone, through the hotel's website, or with an email that reads something like this:

Dear Hotel Central,
I would like to reserve a double room for 2 people for 3 nights, arriving 19 July and departing 22 July. If possible, I would like a quiet room with a double bed (not twin beds), a view of the Acropolis, and a shower (not a tub). Please let me know if you have a room available and the price. Thank you.

If they require your credit-card number for a deposit, you can send it by email (I do), but it's safer via phone, the hotel's secure website, or split between two emails. Once your room is booked, print out the confirmation, and reconfirm your reservation with a phone call or email a day or two in advance (alert them if you'll be arriving after 17:00). If canceling a reservation, some hotels require advance notice—otherwise they may bill you. Even if there's no penalty, it's polite to give at least three days' notice.

Budget Tips

Because of the economic situation in Greece, you'll find good values and soft prices. Comparison-shop by checking prices at several hotels (on each hotel's own website, on a booking site, or by email). For the best deal, book directly with the hotel. Many hotels offer a discount to those who pay cash or stay longer than three nights. To cut costs further, try asking for a cheaper room (for example, with a shared bathroom or no window) or offer to skip breakfast. Additionally, some accommodations offer a special discount for Rick Steves readers.

You'll pay a premium to stay near the Acropolis. Many hotels have Acropolis-view rooms—some for no extra charge, but usually for a higher rate.

Don't be too cheap when picking a hotel. In summer, pay a little more for air-conditioning. And remember that cheaper places in boring neighborhoods can be depressing. Your Athens experience will be more memorable with a welcoming oasis to call home.

PLAKA AND SYNTAGMA NEIGHBORHOODS
Predictable business-class comfort near the old center

$$$ Hotel Plaka Kapnikarea 7 tel. 210-322-2096, www.plakahotel.gr	Business hotel with rooftop bar/terrace and modern rooms (some with Acropolis views)
$$$ Hermes Hotel Apollonos 19 tel. 210-323-5514, www.hermeshotel.gr	Same owners as Hotel Plaka, but better value and newer rooms on a quiet street close to Syntagma; RS discount
$$$ Central Hotel Apollonos 21 tel. 210-323-4357, www.centralhotel.gr	Sleek rooms with an anonymous vibe; some rooms have balconies and views
$$$ Hotel Grande Bretagne Vassileos Georgiou 1 tel. 210-333-0000, www.grandebretagne.gr	Five-star splurge with 19th-century elegance; ranks among the grand hotels of the world
$$$ Hotel Electra Palace Nikodimou 18 tel. 210-337-0000, www.electrahotels.gr	Luxury hotel in a nondescript urban zone with plush rooms and snooty service; Acropolis-view outdoor pool
$$ Hotel Acropolis House Kodrou 6 tel. 210-322-2344, www.acropolishouse.gr	Homey villa filled with antiques and dark-wood furnishings, pay in cash, no elevator
$$ Niki Hotel Nikis 27 tel. 210-322-0913, www.nikihotel.gr	New Age hotel with tight-but-trendy rooms and reasonable rates
$$ Hotel Adonis Kodrou 3 tel. 210-324-9737, www.hotel-adonis.gr	On the quiet, traffic-free upper reaches of Kodrou; fourth-floor rooms have good views of the Acropolis
$$ Pan Hotel Mitropoleos 11 tel. 210-323-7816, www.panhotel.gr	Centrally located, just below Syntagma Square; ancient but well-maintained rooms
$ Hotel Kimon Apollonos 27 tel. 210-331-4658, www.kimonhotel.com	Crank-'em-out hotel with well-appointed rooms; no elevator

$ Hotel Phaedra Herefondos 16 tel. 210-323-8461, www.hotelphaedra.com	Simple but wonderfully located hotel two blocks from Hadrian's Arch; breakfast extra
$ Student & Travellers' Inn Kidathineon 16 tel. 210-324-4808, www.studenttravellersinn.com	Plaka's best backpacker hostel, with recently renovated rooms; breakfast extra
$ Athens International Youth Hostel (a.k.a. "Hotel Victor Hugo") 16 Victor Hugo tel. 210-523-2540, www.athens-international.com	High-rise hostel just outside the tourist zone near the Metaxourghio Metro stop

PSYRRI NEIGHBORHOOD
Emerging nightlife and dining district just north of Monastiraki

$$$ Athens Center Square Hotel Aristogitonos 15 tel. 210-321-1770, www.athenscentersquarehotel.gr	Comfortable home base amid market action; roof garden with Acropolis views; RS discount
$$ Hotel Cecil Athinas 39 tel. 210-321-7079, www.cecil.gr	Conveniently located on the edge of Psyrri in a lightly updated old building
$$ Hotel Attalos Athinas 29 tel. 210-321-2801, www.attaloshotel.com	Tired but peaceful budget standby with Acropolis views from roof; breakfast extra
$ Hotel Phidias Apostolou Pavlou 39 tel. 210-345-9511, www.phidias.gr	Right on the Apostolou Pavlou pedestrian drag with dated but reasonably priced rooms
$ Hotel Tempi Aiolou 29 tel. 210-321-3175, www.tempihotel.gr	Spartan rooms and cramped bathrooms on lively Agia Irini Square (with cafés and bars); elevator for luggage only; breakfast at café next door extra

Sleeping

MAKRIGIANNI AND KOUKAKI NEIGHBORHOODS Residential area behind the Acropolis	
$$$ Hotel Hera Falirou 9 tel. 210-923-6682, www.herahotel.gr	Great value near the Acropolis, with plush rooms above classy lobby
$$$ Hotel Acropolis Select Falirou 37 tel. 210-921-1610, www.acropoliselect.gr	Well-run hotel with can-do staff, generous breakfast, and stylish lobby
$$ Art Gallery Hotel Erecthiou 5 tel. 210-923-8376, www.artgalleryhotel.gr	Comfy hotel near the top of a pleasant stair-step lane; breakfast extra
$$ Athens Studios Veikou 3A tel. 210-923-5811, www.athensstudios.gr	Well-appointed, good-value apartments with kitchens and nice touches
$ Marble House Zini 35a tel. 210-923-4058, www.marblehouse.gr	Family-run place with cared-for rooms; breakfast extra, air-con extra, no elevator
$ Athens Backpackers Makri 12 tel. 210-922-4044, www.backpackers.gr	Youthful and fun-loving, with good bunks and two on-site bars; well-run by gregarious Aussies

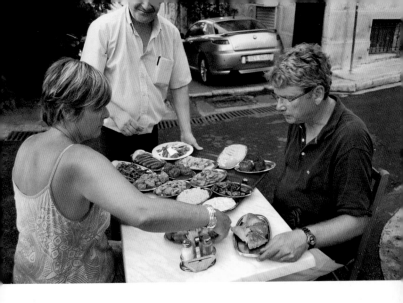

Eating

Greek food is simple...and simply delicious. There's little point in seeking out trendy, non-Greek eateries. Locals and tourists alike fill endless tavernas, *mezedopolios* (eateries selling small plates called *mezedes*—known internationally as *meze*), *ouzeries* (bars selling ouzo liquor and pub grub), and other traditional eateries dishing up the basics.

I've listed restaurants by neighborhood (see the maps on pages 153-155). You probably won't be able to resist dining in the Plaka one night, but in that very touristy area, prices are high and quality is mixed. Gazi and Psyrri—very different but equally worthwhile dining zones—are a short walk beyond the Plaka. I've also listed good options near the Acropolis Museum, in Makrigianni and Koukaki.

Restaurant Price Code

$$$ Most main courses €25 or more; fine dining.
$$ Most main courses €15-25; nice but not too fancy.
$ Most main courses €15 or less; unpretentious yet tasty.

Based on the average price of a meat or seafood dish. Salads and *mezedes* are several euros cheaper. So a typical meal in a $$ restaurant—including *mezedes*, main dish, house wine, water, and service—would cost about €40. The circled numbers in the restaurant listings indicate locations on the maps on pages 153-155.

Athenians like to eat late (dinnertime is typically 21:00-24:00). When you sit down, you'll be asked if you want a basket of bread, often with napkins and flatware tucked inside (a bread and cover charge of €0.50-1 is standard). Menus are usually in Greek and English. Many tavernas will have a display case showing what they've been cooking for the day, and it's perfectly acceptable to ask for a look and point to the dish you want. Bring cash; credit cards aren't always accepted. For tips on tipping, see page 163. Smoking is banned in enclosed spaces, such as restaurants and bars, so smokers sit outside. Despite the law, many bars and some restaurants allow smoking inside, too.

Greek Cuisine

The four Greek food groups are olives (and olive oil), salty feta cheese, tasty tomatoes, and crispy phyllo dough. Virtually every dish is based upon these four building blocks.

Greeks are justly proud of their olive oil: Their country is the third-largest producer in the EU, and they consume almost seven gallons per person a year. Common, edible Greek olives include the purple and almond-shaped *kalamata*; black, wrinkled *throubes*; and large green *halkithiki* (often stuffed).

The best-known Greek cheese is feta, varying from soft, moist, and mild, to sour, hard, and crumbly. Other cheeses include mild, yellow *kasseri* and sweet, nutty *graviera*.

Flaky phyllo-dough pastries called "pies" (*pita,* not to be confused with pita bread) can be starters in restaurants or purchased from a bakery for a tasty bite to go. Look for *spanakopita* (spinach), *tiropita* (cheese), *kreatopita* (beef or pork), *meletzanitopita* (eggplant), and *bougatsa* (with a sweet cream filling).

Small plates called *mezedes* (meh-ZEH-dehs) are a great way to sample several foods. The most common is Greek salad (a.k.a. *horiatiki,* "village" salad), with chopped tomatoes, rich feta cheese (in a long slab that you break apart with your fork), olives, and onions, all drenched with olive oil. Other typical *mezedes* are *pantzarosalata* (beet salad), *bekri meze* ("drunkard's snack"—chicken, pork, or beef cooked with wine, cloves, cinnamon, and bay leaves), *dolmathes* (grape or cabbage leaves stuffed with meat or rice), *taramosalata* (fish-roe dip), and *saganaki* (fried cheese).

My favorite snack is souvlaki pita—grilled meat (often pork or chicken) wrapped in pita bread. Souvlaki goes well with *tzatziki,* a thick, garlicky yogurt-and-cucumber sauce. Souvlaki stands are all over Greece. Just order and pay at the cashier, then take your receipt to the counter to claim your meal. Souvlaki places also sell hearty Greek salads and plates of meat shaved from gyros (cooked by stacking meat on a metal skewer and vertically slow-roasting it), along with wine, beer, and ouzo to wash it down.

Casseroles include the classic moussaka, with layers of minced meat, eggplant, and potatoes under cheesy béchamel sauce or egg custard; and its meat-and-pasta cousin *pastitsio* ("Greek lasagna"). *Arnaki kleftiko* is slow-cooked lamb wrapped in phyllo dough or parchment paper, while *stifado* is beef stew with onions, tomatoes, cinnamon, and cloves.

Gavros is a seafood appetizer similar to anchovies—drizzle with lemon juice, and eat everything but the little tails. Marinated and grilled octopus is *htapothi;* grilled or fried red mullet is *barbounia. Psari plaki* is fish baked in the oven with tomatoes and onions.

For dessert, look for baklava (phyllo dough layered with nuts and honey), *kataifi* (thin phyllo fibers—like shredded wheat—layered with nuts and honey), *ekmek* (custard-/whipped-cream-topped cake made of honey-soaked phyllo fibers), or *loukoumades* (honey-soaked doughnuts).

Water, generally cheap and rarely carbonated, is served in bottles. There are two basic types of Greek wines: retsina (resin-flavored, rarely served) and nonresinated wines. Retsina wine, a post-WWII rotgut with a notorious resin flavor, has long been famous as the working man's Greek wine. If pine sap is not your cup of tea, there are plenty of other wine options. With its new generation of winemakers (many of them trained abroad), Greece is receiving more recognition for its wines. Beer is mostly imported, but you will find local brands (Alpha, Fix, Vergina, and Mythos). Cloudy, anise-flavored ouzo and the even-better tsipouro brandy are worth a try, and rich, golden-colored Metaxa liqueur is for after dinner.

If you want good local coffee for half the price of Starbucks and want your money to stay in Greece, you'll find handy branches of Grigoris Coffee Right (a Greek gourmet coffee chain) all over town. They serve cheap but fancy coffee and offer all the light bites, pastries, and trendy ambience you need. The Mikel Coffee chain is a bit pricier and more posh. In summer, Greeks sip iced coffee drinks. *Freddo cappuccino* (iced cappuccino) is the drink of choice, though you will also usually find the frappé (iced Nescafé; order it black or white—with milk), *freddo espresso* (iced espresso), and *freddo Mokka.* Tavernas and some cafés still serve traditional Greek coffee, made with loose grounds.

THE PLAKA
Avoid the touristy joints on the main drag and head for the more authentic-feeling places on the quieter hillside above, including the stepped lane called Mnisikleous and the streets nearby

❶	**$$ Xenios Zeus** (ΞΕΝΙΟΣ ΖΕΥΣ) Mnisikleous 37 tel. 210-324-9514	Proudly set at the top of the Mnisikleous steps, with good, traditional Greek food inside or out on a terrace (daily 11:00-24:00, closed Nov-March)
❷	**$$ Geros tou Moria Tavern** Mnisikleous 27 tel. 210-322-1753	Venerable place, with a dining hall, intimate terrace, and tables under the grapevines (daily 12:00-24:00)
❸	**$$ Palia Taverna tou Psara** ("The Old Tavern of Psaras") Eretheos 16 tel. 210-321-8734	A big, slick, dish-'em-up eatery with live folk music in lower building and grand rooftop terrace (daily 12:00-24:00)
❹	**$ Scholarhio Ouzeri Kouklis Mezedes** Tripodon 14 tel. 210-324-7605	Waiters present a big platter of fun, inexpensive *mezedes*—you choose; lively front terrace and romantic balconies for two; free homemade ouzo with this book (daily 11:00-24:00)

⑤	**$ Klepsidra Café** Thrasivoulou 9 tel. 210-321-2493	Serves light bites, good desserts, traditional coffee, and lots of booze to a young local crowd at tiny tables littering ramshackle steps (daily 9:00-24:00)
⑥	**$$ Brettos Distillery** Kidathineon 41 tel. 210-323-2100	Oldest distillery in Athens (1909), buried in the heart of the Plaka kitsch, with shots and wines by the glass served under huge old casks (daily 10:00-24:00)
NEAR MONASTIRAKI SQUARE The go-to area for cheap souvlaki		
⑦	**$ "Souvlaki Row"** Monastiraki Square (where it meets Mitropoleos street)	Souvlaki heaven, with three frantic restaurants—Thanasis, Savvas, and Bairaktaris—spilling into the street and serving food to-go or at a table (daily until very late)
⑧	**$ Kosta Souvlaki** Agia Irini Square, off Aiolou street	Beloved hole-in-the-wall that's been serving traditional and cheap skewer-roasted souvlaki since the 1940s (daily 9:00-17:00)
NEAR SYNTAGMA SQUARE Urban dining on and near Athens' main square		
⑨	**$$ O Tzitzikas ki o Mermigkas** ("The Ant and the Cricket") Mitropoleos 12 tel. 210-324-7607	Modern regional cuisine served at sidewalk tables or indoors in a fun, retro-grocery-store atmosphere (daily 13:00-24:00)
⑩	**$$ Athinaikon Restaurant** Mitropoleos 34 tel. 210-325-2688	A venerable businessman's favorite, serving a variety of traditional *mezedes* and Greek and Mediterranean recipes (Mon-Sat 12:00-24:00, Sun until 19:00)
⑪	**$$$ 2Mazi Restaurant Wine Bar** Nikis 48 tel. 210-322-2839	Modern Greek gourmet cooking in a stylish setting with equally stylish locals (daily 13:00-24:00, reservations smart, www.2mazi.gr)
⑫	**$$$ Hotel Grande Bretagne's Roof Garden Restaurant** On Syntagma Square tel. 210-333-0766	Athens' finest dining experience and a swanky bar, on a rooftop garden with spectacular Acropolis/city views; dress code (daily 13:00-24:00, reservations required for meals, www.grandebretagne.gr)

Eating

⓭	**$$ By the Glass Wine Bar** Y. Souri 3 tel. 210-323-2560	A jazz-cool, relaxed place where you can learn about Greek wines and enjoy plates of mixed Greek cheeses, meats, and upscale nibbles (daily 12:00-24:00)
⓮	**$ Kimolia Art Café** (Κιμωλία) Ypereidou 5 tel. 211-184-8446	A cute little pastel place serving light café fare with reasonable prices and a relaxing vibe (daily 10:00-late)
⓯	**$ Avocado Vegetarian Café** Nikis 30 tel. 210-323-7878	Yoga-friendly eatery with lots of energy juices, a passion for organic farming, and nothing with eyeballs (Mon-Sat 11:00-22:00, Sun 12:00-19:00)
⓰	**$ Ariston** (ΑΡΙΣΤΟΝ) Voulis 10 tel. 210-322-7626	Cheapest hot meal in town; Athens' top spot for savory and sweet pastries such as *spanakopita* (spinach pie) and *tiropita* (cheese pie; open Mon-Sat 7:30-18:00 plus Tue and Thu-Fri until 21:00, closed Sun)
⓱	**$ Konstantinidis** Stadiou 3 (Second location in Koukaki at Syngrou Ave. 98)	A local favorite for ice cream and baklava that embraces its "good old days" heritage

PSYRRI AND NEARBY
Thriving nightlife district with eateries concentrated near Iroon and Agii Anargiri squares and the Central Market

⓲	**$ Taverna tou Psyrri** Eschilou 12 tel. 210-321-4923	Old and authentic-feeling, with checkerboard tablecloths, garden terrace in back, straightforward menu, and good prices (daily 12:00-24:00)
⓳	**$ O Nikitas** (Ο Νικήτας) Agion Anargyron 19 tel. 210-325-2591	Serves mainly *mezedes* and good food to a local crowd on a peaceful square (daily 12:00-18:00 plus Wed-Sat until 23:00)
⓴	**$ Avli** (αυλή) Agiou Dimitriou 12 (small doorway labeled αυλή)	A long, skinny, and thriving courtyard with a jumble of tiny tables, serving a daily *meze* plate (daily 12:00-24:00)

21	**$ Ta Karamanlidika** Evripidou 52 tel. 210-325-4184	A quality meat-and-cheese shop that doubles as a restaurant, with a mix of Byzantine and Cappadocian flavors, aged cheese, and cured meats (Mon-Sat 12:00-23:00, closed Sun)
22	**$$ James Joyce Irish Pub** Astiggos 12 tel. 210-323-5055	Woody escape from Greece with Irish-pub ambience and menu, and top Irish beers on tap (daily until late)
23	**$ Central Market** 500 yards north of Monastiraki Square on Athinas street	Great place to assemble a cheap picnic of fruits, veggies, olives, cheeses, nuts, meats, and fish (Mon-Sat 7:00–15:00, closed Sun)
24	**$ Karayiannis Ouzo Bar** In Central Market (on side aisle, midway down the fish section)	Great place for an ouzo and *mezedes* while enjoying the Central Market action (Mon-Sat 7:30-15:00, closed Sun)
25	**$ Koulouri of Psyrri** Karaiskaki 23 tel. 210-321-5962	Serves oven-fresh sesame bread rings, a popular Athenian on-the-run snack sold at corner carts throughout the city
26	**$ Bougatsadiko Thessaloniki** 1 Iroon Square tel. 210-322-2088	A bakery where you can watch the pastry master at work and sample some of the city's best *bougatsa*—thin pastry with cream inside
27	**$ Krinos** 87 Aiolou tel. 210-321-6852	Famed for its *loukoumades*—doughnuts soaked in honey or sugar syrup (closed Sun)
28	**$ Mokka Coffee** 44 Athinas tel. 210-321-6892	Good spot for a Greek coffee made the traditional way—water, grounds, and sugar slowly heated in a tray of hot sand

GAZI
Trendy, artsy, and gay-friendly former industrial zone at the western edge of Athens' tourist zone

㉙	**$$ Kazani Meze Restaurant** Persefonis 39 tel. 210-346-4984	Stylish place that's sleek yet classic, serving an enjoyable and accessible menu of *mezedes* (daily 13:00-24:00)
㉙	**$ Kandavlos Souvlaki** Persefonis 47 tel. 210-342-4725	Thriving student hangout with white tables and a clubby crowd, with the best cheap souvlaki in Gazi (daily 11:00-24:00)
㉙	**$ Gazi College Eatery** Persefonis 53 tel. 210-342-2112	Fresh and inviting place for a light meal or drink in the company of university students (daily 8:00-24:00)

MAKRIGIANNI AND KOUKAKI
Pair of neighborhoods near the Acropolis Museum, filled with tourist-friendly eateries

㉚	**$$ Mani Mani** Falirou 10 (upstairs) tel. 210-921-8180	A touch of class at reasonable prices, with cuisine from the Mani Peninsula and all-indoor seating (daily 14:00-23:00 in summer, shorter hours in winter, reservations smart, www.manimani.com.gr)
㉛	**$$ Strofi Athenian Restaurant** Rovertou Galli 25 tel. 210-921-4130	My favorite for white-tablecloth, elegantly modern, rooftop-Acropolis-view dining (Tue-Sun 12:00-late, closed Mon, reservations smart, www.strofi.gr)
㉜	**$ To Kati Allo Restaurant** Chatzichristou 12 tel. 210-922-3071	Quintessential hole-in-the-wall on far side of the Acropolis Museum; blackboard menu lists cheap, fresh options (daily 11:00-24:00)

Makrigianni & Koukaki Restaurants

Restaurants in Central Athens & Psyrri

SOFOKLEOUS

27 To Omonia Square, National Archaeological Museum & Exarchia

ARISTEIDOU

DRAGAT-SANIOU

AYII THEODOROI

PRAXITELOUS

AYIOU MARKOU

MILTIA DOU

NIKOU

KALAMIOTOU

EVANG

ROMVIS

THISEOS

PAPARIGOPOULOU

Panepistimio Ⓜ

EDOUARDOU LO

OMIROU

MUSEUM OF THE CITY OF ATHENS

KARITZI

ANTHIMOS

OLD PARLIAMENT

AMERIKIS

PANEPISTIMIOU

ELEFTHERIOU VENIZELOU

VOUKOURESTIOU

LYKAVITTOU

KRIEZOTOU

ZALOKOSTA

KOLOKOTRONI

LEKKA

VOULIS

STADIOU

16

SYNTAGMA

17

HOTEL GRANDE BRETAGNE

12

To Kolonaki & Lykavittos Hill

ATHINAIDOS

CHURCH OF KAPNIKAREA

MONASTIRAKI

PERIKLEOUS

KARA. SERV.

VAS. SOFIAS

Ⓜ Syntagma

FOKIONOS

MITROPOLEOS

PETRAKI

SKOPA

VAS.GEORGIOU

Ⓑ Bus #X80 to/from Piraeus

Ⓜ Syntagma

TOMB OF THE UNKNOWN SOLDIER

PANDROSSOU

CATHEDRAL

Cathedral (MITROPOLIS) Square

10

AGIOS ELEFTHERIOS

ERMOU

9

MITROPOLEOS

POST

Syntagma Square

OTHONOS

Ⓜ Syntagma

PARLIAMENT

APOLLONOS

IPITOU

VOULIS

SKOUFOU

NIKIS

FILELLINON

Ⓑ Bus #040 to Piraeus

XENOFONDOS

Ⓑ Bus #X95 to Airport

Ⓜ Syntagma

DIOGENOUS

ERETHEOS

KYRRISTOU

ADRIANOU

AG. FILOTHEIS

AG. FILOTHEIS

NIKODIMOU

15

14

Y. SOURI

13

LISSIOU

FLESSA

IPERIDOU

11

JEWISH MUSEUM

PSYLI

National Garden

PRYTANIOU

TRIPODON

SKHOLIOU

SOTIROS

PLAKA

ADRIANOU

VASILISSIS AMALIAS

AG. GEORGIOS

4

KYDATHINEON

DEDALOU

ZAPPEION (EXHIBITION HALL)

STRATONOS

THESPIDOS

KANGAVA

SHELLY

6

AG. AIKATERINI

Filomousou Square

THOLOU

Practicalities

Helpful Websites

Greece's Tourist Information: www.visitgreece.gr

Athens Info: Hellenic Ministry of Culture & Tourism (www.culture.gr), City of Athens Convention and Visitors Bureau (www.thisisathens.org), Matt Barrett's Athens Survival Guide (www.athensguide.com)

Cheap Flights: Olympic (www.olympicair.com), Aegean (www.aegeanair.com), or try www.kayak.com

Greek Bus Help (unofficial): http://livingingreece.gr (under "Best of..." click on "KTEL Buses of Greece")

Ferry Schedules for Greek Islands: www.gtp.gr, www.danae.gr/ferries-Greece.asp, www.greekferries.gr

General Travel Tips: www.ricksteves.com (trip planning, packing lists, and more—plus updates for this book)

PLANNING

When to Go

Late spring and fall are pleasant, with comfortable weather, no rain, and lighter crowds (except during holiday weekends). In summer, Athens is packed with tourists, and hotel prices can be high. July and August are the hottest months. Late October through mid-March is colder and can be rainy: During these months, some sights close for lunch and some tourist activities vanish altogether. Off-season hotel rates are soft; look for bargains.

Before You Go

Make sure your passport is up to date (to renew, see www.travel.state.gov). Call your debit- and credit-card companies about your plans (see below). Book rooms well in advance if you'll be traveling during peak season or any major holidays. Consider buying travel insurance (see www.ricksteves.com/insurance). If traveling beyond Athens, research transit schedules (buses, ferries) and car rentals. If renting a car, bring your driver's license and an International Driving Permit (sold at your local AAA office), though I've often rented cars in Greece without one.

MONEY

Greece uses the euro currency: 1 euro (€) = about $1.10. To convert prices in euros to dollars, add about 10 percent: €20 = about $22, €50 = about $55 (bills over €50 are rarely used). (Check www.oanda.com for the latest exchange rates.)

Cash is highly preferable in Greece. Small businesses (some hotels, mom-and-pop cafés, shops, etc.) may require payment in cash. Withdraw money from a cash machine using a debit card, just like at home. Visa and MasterCard are commonly used throughout Europe. Before departing, call your bank and credit-card company: Confirm that your card will work overseas, ask about international transaction fees, and alert them that you'll be making withdrawals in Europe. Many travelers bring a second debit/credit card as a backup. Try to withdraw large sums of money to reduce the number of per-transaction bank fees you'll pay.

While American magnetic-stripe credit cards and newer chip-embedded cards are accepted almost everywhere in Europe, they may not work in some payment machines (e.g., ticket kiosks) geared for European-style chip-and-PIN cards. Be prepared to pay with cash, try entering your card's PIN, or find a nearby cashier.

To keep your cash and valuables safe, wear a money belt. But if you do lose your credit or debit card, report the loss immediately. Call these 24-hour US numbers collect: Visa (303/967-1096), MasterCard (636/722-7111), and American Express (336/393-1111).

ARRIVAL IN ATHENS

Eleftherios Venizelos International Airport

Athens' airport is at Spata, 17 miles east of downtown (airport code: ATH, tel. 210-353-0000, www.aia.gr). B gates serve European/Schengen countries (no passport control), while A gates cover other destinations, including the US. Both sections feed into a main terminal building (with baggage claim, ATMs, shops, car-rental counters, and info desks).

To get between the airport and downtown Athens, you have several options:

Metro: Line 3/blue zips you downtown (Syntagma or Monastiraki stop) in 45 minutes (€8, ticket good for 70 minutes on other Athens transit,

Athens Transit

Metro Line 1
Metro Line 2
Metro Line 3
Bus Line w/#
Rail
Coastal Tram w/#

Trains to
Thessaloniki &
Northern Greece

Kifissia

Irini

Bus
Terminal B
(Liosion)

Anthoupoli

To
Piraeus ←

#X96

AIRPORT

Aghia
Marina

Larissis
(Train Stn.)

Attiki

NATIONAL
ARCHAEOLOGICAL
MUSEUM

Egaleo

Victoria

Bus Terminal A
(Kifissou)

Kera-
mikos

Omonia

#051

LYKAVITTOS
HILL

To
Airport

Monastiraki

Evangelismos

#X95

#X96

Thissio

ACROPOLIS

Syntagma

Akropoli

Syngrou-Fix

Piraeus

Neo
Faliro

#040 & #X80

Neos Kosmos

CRUISE
PORT

NEA
SMYRNI

N

1 & 2

Helliniko

Ferries &
Hydrofoils
to Islands

Saronic
Gulf

2

To Voula

DCH
Not to Scale

2/hour, direction: Agia Marina, daily 6:30-23:30). From the main terminal, use exit #3, cross the street, go up the escalator, and cross the skybridge to the rail terminal. Buy tickets (machines take cash only), and follow signs to the platforms. Stamp your ticket in a validation machine before you board.

Bus: Express bus #X95 operates 24 hours daily between the airport and Syntagma Square (3-5/hour, 1 hour, €5, catch it outside exit #5, tel. 185, www.oasa.gr).

Taxi: A taxi stand outside exit #3 offers fixed-price transfers that include all fees (€38 to central Athens).

Port of Piraeus

Piraeus, six miles southwest of central Athens, is the main port for cruise ships and boats to/from the Greek islands. The easy, cheap way to get between the port and central Athens is by Metro. Line 1/green links Piraeus with the Monastiraki stop in downtown Athens in about 20 minutes (watch for pickpockets on this line, and wear a money belt). Transfer at Omonia for Syntagma, Akropoli, and Syngrou-Fix Metro stops.

A taxi between central Athens and Piraeus costs €15-20 (surcharges apply) and takes 20-40 minutes, depending on traffic and start/end points.

Cruise-ship passengers unload at the far-south end of the port. Because the Metro station is a 20-40-minute walk from here, ask at the terminal about public bus #X80 or #040 or one of the hop-on, hop-off buses that goes to Athens (www.citysightseeing.gr or www.athensopentour.com).

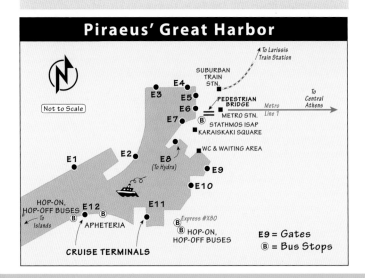

Piraeus' Great Harbor

To Larissis / Train Station

SUBURBAN TRAIN STN.

E4
E3
E5
PEDESTRIAN BRIDGE

To Central Athens

Metro Line 1

E6
E7
METRO STN.
Ⓑ STATHMOS ISAP
KARAISKAKI SQUARE

Not to Scale

E1
E2
E8
(To Hydra)

WC & WAITING AREA

E9

E10

HOP-ON, HOP-OFF BUSES
To Islands

E12
Ⓑ   Ⓑ
APHETERIA

E11

Ⓑ Express #X80
Ⓑ HOP-ON, HOP-OFF BUSES

E9 = Gates
Ⓑ = Bus Stops

CRUISE TERMINALS

Bus Stations

Athens' two major bus stations—Kifissou (Terminal A) and Liosion (Terminal B)—are far from downtown and lack convenient Metro connections.

Terminal A, about three miles northwest of the city center, serves buses from the south, including the Peloponnese. To reach central Athens, it's easiest to take a taxi (pay no more than €15).

Terminal B, which serves Delphi and other destinations in the north, is about a 15-minute, €8 taxi ride to the Plaka.

Larissis Train Station

Most trains use Larissis Station, just north of downtown (on Metro line 2/red). Greek trains are of limited usefulness to travelers. The train does serves areas north of Athens well (such as Thessaloniki), but is essentially useless if connecting south to the Peloponnese.

HELPFUL HINTS

Tourist Information (TI): The Greek National Tourist Organization (EOT), with its main branch near the Acropolis Museum, covers Athens and the rest of the country. Although their advice can be hit-or-miss, it's worth a stop to pick up their free city map, pocket public transportation map, *Athens Live* booklet, and their slick, glossy book on Athens. They also have information on museums and hours, entertainment options, and bus and train connections (April-Sept Mon-Fri 8:00-20:00, Sat-Sun 10:00-16:00; Oct-March Mon-Fri 9:00-19:00 or possibly earlier, Sat-Sun 10:00-16:00; on pedestrian street leading to Acropolis Museum at Dionysiou Areopagitou 18, Metro: Akropoli; tel. 210-331-0392, www.visitgreece.gr, info@gnto.gr).

Hurdling the Language Barrier: Although the Greek alphabet presents challenges to foreign visitors, communication is not hard. Most people in the tourist industry—and virtually all young people—speak English. Many signs and menus use both the Greek and Latin alphabets. For Greek survival phrases, see page 173.

Time Zones: Greece is generally one hour ahead of continental Europe and seven/ten hours ahead of the East/West Coasts of the US.

Watt's Up? Europe's electrical system is 220 volts, instead of North America's 110 volts. Most newer electronics (including hair dryers, laptops, and battery chargers) convert automatically, so you won't need a

Tipping

Tipping in Europe isn't as automatic and generous as it is in the US. At Greek restaurants that have waitstaff, service is generally included, although it's common to round up the bill after a good meal (about 10 percent). To tip a taxi driver, round up your fare (for instance, if the fare is €4.50, pay €5). In general, if someone in the service industry does a super job for you, a small tip of a euro or two is appropriate...but not required.

voltage converter—but you will need a special adapter plug with two round prongs, sold inexpensively at US and Canadian travel stores.

Numbers and Stumblers: What Americans call the second floor of a building is the first floor in Europe. Europeans write dates as day/month/year, so Christmas is 25/12/17. Commas are decimal points and vice versa—a dollar and a half is 1,50, and there are 5.280 feet in a mile.

Greece uses the metric system: A kilogram is 2.2 pounds; a liter is about a quart; and a kilometer is six-tenths of a mile. Temperature is measured in Celsius. 0°C = 32°F. To convert Celsius to Fahrenheit, double the number and add 30.

Holidays: Many sights and banks close down on national holidays. Verify dates through the Greek National Tourist Organization (www.visitgreece.gr), or check www.ricksteves.com/festivals.

Pedestrian Safety: Streets that appear to be "traffic-free" often are shared by motorcycles or mopeds. Don't step into any street without looking both ways. Athens' marble-like streets and red pavement tiles can become very slick when it rains. Watch your step.

Internet Access: Bits and Bytes is in the heart of the Plaka (open 24 hours daily, just off Agora Square at Kapnikareas 19, tel. 210-325-3142).

Bookshops: Eleftheroudakis (ΕΛΕΥΘΕΡΟΥΔΑΚΗΣ) is Greece's answer to Barnes & Noble, with a great selection of travel guides and maps, along with a lot of English books (Mon-Fri 9:00-21:00, Sat 9:00-16:00, closed Sun, three blocks north of Syntagma Square at Panepistimiou/Eleftheriou Venizelou 15, tel. 210-305-8440). **Public** at Syntagma Square offers a reasonable variety of English books (tel. 210-324-6210).

Laundry: A full-service launderette is in the Plaka (closed Sat-Sun,

Practicalities

Apollonos 17, tel. 210-323-2226). **Athens Studios,** in the Makrigianni neighborhood, operates a self-service launderette (daily, Veikou 3A, tel. 210-922-4044).

GETTING AROUND ATHENS

Because the tourists' core of Athens is so walkable, most travelers don't need the Metro or buses, other than for reaching farther-flung destinations (such as the airport or National Archaeological Museum). For information on all of Athens' public transportation, see www.oasa.gr. Beware of pickpockets.

Buying Tickets

Purchase tickets at machines or from ticket windows. The basic ticket (€1.20, half price if over 65 or under 18) is good for 70 minutes on all public transit, including the Metro, buses, and trams, and covers transfers (pricier €8 ticket required for airport). A 24-hour ticket is €4; a five-day ticket costs €10 (neither includes airport). If starting and finishing at the airport, consider the three-day tourist ticket (€20), which includes a round-trip airport transfer on the Metro or Express bus #X95 as well as unlimited in-city public-transit travel.

By Metro

The Metro is the most straightforward way to get around. Trains run every few minutes on weekdays and slightly less frequently on weekends (5:00-24:00, later on Fri-Sat, www.stasy.gr). To avoid a hefty fine, stamp your ticket in a validation machine—usually located near the ticket booth—before you board (multiride tickets only need to be stamped the first time).

Athens has three Metro lines. The older and slower **Line 1** (green) stops at Piraeus (boats to the islands), Thissio (good restaurants and nightlife), Monastiraki (city center), Victoria (10-minute walk from National Archaeological Museum), and Omonia (15-minute walk from National Archaeological Museum). Key **Line 2** (red) stops include Larissis (train station), Syntagma (city center), Omonia (National Archaeological Museum), Akropoli (Acropolis and Makrigianni/Koukaki hotel neighborhood), and Syngrou-Fix (Makrigianni/Koukaki hotels). **Line 3** (blue) stops at Keramikos (near Gazi), Monastiraki and Syntagma (city center), Evangelismos

(Kolonaki museum neighborhood), and the airport (requires a separate ticket—see page 159).

By Bus

Validate tickets in the orange machines as you board (buy tickets in advance, either from a special ticket kiosk or at a Metro station—you cannot buy tickets from the driver). In general, I'd avoid the slow, crowded buses, with these exceptions: bus #035 (from Athinas street, near Monastiraki, to National Archaeological Museum); bus #224 (from Syntagma Square to National Archaeological Museum); bus #X95 (from airport to Syntagma Square); and bus #X96 (from airport to Piraeus). Bus info: www.oasa.gr.

By Taxi

Despite the vulgar penchant some cabbies here have for ripping off tourists (especially at the cruise terminals), Athens is a great taxi town. Its yellow taxis are cheap and handy (€3.50 minimum charge covers most short rides in town; after that, it's €0.74/km—tariff 1 on the meter, plus tolls, fees for bags over 10 kilograms/22 pounds, and surcharges for trips to/from the train and bus stations, and Piraeus; airport fee included in airport flat rate). You'll pay 50 percent more between midnight and 5:00 in the morning and outside the city limits (tariff 2). Hotels and restaurants can order a taxi ("radio taxi"), but there's a €2-4 surcharge (if cabbies try to charge more than that, hold firm). **Uber** is also an option for people who use it at home.

STAYING CONNECTED

Telephones and Internet

Making Calls: To call Greece from the US or Canada: Dial 011 (our international access code), then 30 (Greece's country code), and then the local number. To call Greece from a European country: Dial 00 (Europe's international access code), then 30 followed by the local number. If you're calling from a mobile phone, you can enter a + instead of 00 or 011 (press and hold the 0 key). To call within Greece, just dial the local number. To call from Greece to another country: Dial 00, the country code (for example, 1 for the US or Canada), the area code and number. If you're calling European countries whose phone numbers begin with 0, you'll usually have to omit that 0 when you dial.

Useful Contacts

Police: tel. 100
Tourist Police: tel. 171 or 1571 (English-speaking)
Medical or Other Emergency: tel. 112
Ambulance: tel. 166
Directory Assistance for Greece: tel. 11888
Directory Assistance for International Calls: tel. 139
US Embassy: tel. 210-720-2414; for after-hours emergency help, tel. 210-729-4444 (consular section open Mon-Fri 8:30-17:00, closed Sat-Sun and last Wed of month)
Canadian Embassy: tel. 210-727-3400; for after-hours emergency help, call Canada collect at tel. 1-613-996-8885 (open Mon-Fri 8:30-12:30, closed Sat-Sun)

Mobile Phones: Many US mobile phones work in Europe. Expect to pay around $1.50 a minute for phone calls, 50 cents to send text messages, and 5 cents to receive them. Most providers offer a global calling plan that cuts the per-minute cost of phone calls and texts, and a flat-fee data plan that includes a certain amount of megabytes.

Unless you have an unlimited-data plan, you're best off saving most of your online tasks for Wi-Fi. You can access the Internet, send texts, and even make voice calls over Wi-Fi. Most hotels offer free Wi-Fi, and you'll also find hotspots at cafés (when you order something, ask the waiter for the Wi-Fi password). To avoid using data roaming on your phone, go to your Settings menu and disable "data roaming" or "cellular data."

You can also buy a phone in Europe, which costs more up front but is cheaper by the call. You'll find mobile-phone stores selling cheap phones (for as little as $20 plus minutes) and SIM cards, at Athens' airport, major train stations, and all over Athens. Or try the electronics store Germanos (ΓΕΡΜΑΜΟΣ).

For more information, talk to your service provider or see www.ricksteves.com/phoning.

Snail Mail

The most convenient post office is at Syntagma Square (open daily, bottom of the square, at corner with Mitropoleos). A smaller neighborhood office is in Makrigianni (Dionysiou Areopagitou 7).

SIGHTSEEING TIPS

Hours: The hours for sights in Greece are often in flux, and with government spending cuts, some sights have reduced hours. I've listed the posted hours, but check locally for the most up-to-date information.

What to Expect: Important sights have metal detectors or conduct bag searches that will slow your entry. Others require you to check (for free) daypacks and coats. To avoid checking a small backpack, carry it under your arm like a purse as you enter. Photos and videos are normally allowed, but flashes or tripods usually are not.

Audioguides and Tours: In Greece, audioguides are rare, but good guidebooks are available.

I've produced free 🎧 audio tours of many of Athens' best sights. With a mobile device, you can take me along as you tour the Acropolis, Ancient Agora, National Archaeological Museum, and the city of Athens itself. You can download Rick Steves Audio Europe via Apple's App Store, Google Play, or the Amazon Appstore.

You can usually hire a live local guide at the entrance to major ancient sites or museums at a reasonable cost (prices are soft and negotiable; save money by splitting the guide fee with other travelers).

Ancient Sites: Archaeological sites are meticulously monitored. Don't cross any barriers or climb on ruins. Posing with ancient statues—or even standing next to them for a photo—is strictly forbidden.

Many major attractions have both an archaeological site and a museum. Visiting the museum (artifacts and scale models) helps you imagine the ruins in their heyday; touring the site gives you the lay of the land. I like to see the site first, but crowds and weather can help determine your plan.

Churches: Many churches have divine art and free entry. Churches encourage a modest dress code (no shorts, bare shoulders, or miniskirts), but few enforce it.

Discounts: Many sights offer discounts for seniors, families, and students or teachers with proper identification cards (www.isic.org). Always ask. Children under 18 sometimes get in for free or cheap. Some discounts are only for EU citizens, but it's worth asking. All museums and archaeological sites run by the Ministry of Greek Culture, including the Acropolis, are free on national holidays and every first Sunday from November through March.

THEFT AND EMERGENCIES

Theft: Be wary of pickpockets, especially in crowds. Avoid carrying a wallet in your back pocket, and hold purses or small day bags in front, particularly at the following locations: Monastiraki flea market, Central Market, changing of the guard at the Tomb of the Unknown Soldier, major public transit routes (such as the Metro between the city and Piraeus), at the port, and on the main streets through the Plaka, such as Adrianou and Pandrossou. I keep my valuables—passport, credit cards, crucial documents, and large amounts of cash—in a money belt that I tuck under my beltline.

If you run into trouble, call the Tourist Police for 24-hour help (tel. 171 or 1571). They serve as a contact point between tourists and other branches of the police and can also handle disputes with hotels and restaurants (office open 24 hours daily, south of the Acropolis in Koukaki at Veikou 43, tel. 210-920-0724).

To replace a passport, you'll need to go in person to an embassy or consulate (for contact info, see page 166). File a police report, either on the spot or within a day or two; it's required to submit an insurance claim for lost or stolen rail passes or travel gear, and it can help with replacing your passport or credit and debit cards. For more information, see www.ricksteves.com/help.

Medical Help: Dial 112 for a medical emergency. If you get sick, do as the locals do and go to a pharmacist for advice. Or ask at your hotel for help—they'll know the nearest medical and emergency services.

ACTIVITIES

Shopping

Most shops catering to tourists are open long hours daily. Those serving locals are open roughly 9:00 to 20:00 on weekdays, have shorter hours on Saturday, and are closed on Sunday. Afternoon breaks are common, and some places close early a few nights a week.

Shopping Neighborhoods: The main streets of the Plaka—especially Adrianou and Pandrossou—are crammed with crass tourist-trap shops (with room to bargain, especially if buying several items).

The famous Monastiraki flea market stretches west of Monastiraki Square, along Ifestou street and its side streets. You'll see plenty of souvenir shops, but the heart of the market is Avissinias Square, filled with antique shops selling furniture, household items, jewelry, dusty books, and knickknacks. There's something going on every day, but the market is best and most crowded on Sundays, when store owners lay out all of the stuff they have been scouting for all week. If buying here, make sure to bargain (Sun flea market open 8:00-15:00, packed with locals by 10:00, Metro: Monastiraki or Thissio).

For upscale shopping at mostly international chain stores, stroll the pedestrianized Ermou street between Syntagma Square and Monastiraki. Many locals prefer the more authentic shops on the streets just to the north, such as Perikleous, Lekka, and Kolokotroni. You can also find upscale fancy boutiques in the swanky Kolonaki area.

What and Where to Buy: Serious buyers tell me that Athens is the best place in Greece to purchase fine jewelry, particularly at the shops along Adrianou (haggling OK). For something a bit more specialized, visit Byzantino for pricey handmade replicas of museum pieces, along with some original designs (Adrianou 120, second location at the corner of Pandrossou and Aiolou). Olympico creates their own modern pieces in the Greek style, along with museum copies. They also sell pieces made by artisans from all over Greece (Adrianou 122).

Melissinos Art, the famous "poet sandal-maker" of Athens, sells handmade leather sandals that you can customize (just off Monastiraki Square at the edge of Psyrri, Ag. Theklas 2).

Icons and other Greek Orthodox objects can make good souvenirs. For the best selection, visit the shops near the cathedral, along Agia Filotheis street (most are closed Sat-Sun).

All over Athens you'll see specialty food stores selling locally produced edibles, such as olive oil, wine and liqueurs, mustards, and sweets like boxed baklava, loukoumi (a.k.a., Greek delight), and jars of "spoon sweets" (jam-like spreads). The best place to shop for these is where the locals do—near the Central Market. Specialty grocers and spice shops cluster around Athinas and Evripidou streets.

Sizes: European clothing sizes are different from those in the US. For example, a woman's size 10 dress (US) is a European size 40, and a size 8 shoe (US) is a European size 38-39.

Getting a VAT Refund: If you spend more than €120 on goods at a single store, you may be eligible to get a refund of the 23 percent Value-Added Tax (VAT). You'll need to ask the merchant to fill out the necessary refund document, and then process your refund through a service such as Global Blue or Premier Tax Free, with offices at major airports. For more details, see www.ricksteves.com/vat.

Customs for American Shoppers: You are allowed to take home $800 worth of items per person duty-free, once every 31 days. You can also bring in a liter of alcohol duty-free. As for food, you can take home many processed and packaged foods (e.g. vacuum-packed cheeses, chocolate, mustard) but no fresh produce or meats. Any liquid-containing foods must be packed (carefully) in checked luggage. To check customs rules and duty rates, visit http://help.cbp.gov.

Entertainment and Nightlife

Athens is a thriving, vibrant city...and Athenians know how to have a good time after hours. For events, look for publications such as the English-language version of the daily newspaper *Kathimerini* (www.ekathimerini.com) and the bimonthly Greek lifestyle magazine *Odyssey* (www.odyssey.gr). Note that although bars are supposed to be nonsmoking, many places don't adhere to this rule. Expect to leave most bars smelling of smoke.

Nightlife Neighborhoods: Your best bet is to get out of the touristy Plaka/Monastiraki rut. A peaceful pedestrian lane circles the Acropolis, providing a delightful place for an evening stroll. This promenade is what I call the "Acropolis Loop" (consisting of Dionysiou Areopagitou to the south and Apostolou Pavlou to the west; see page 122). As the sun goes down, it's busy with locals (lovers, families, seniors, children at play) and visitors alike. The promenade cuts through the Thissio district, just beyond the Agora, where the tables and couches of trendy clubs and cocktail bars clog the pedestrian lanes under the Acropolis.

In seedy-chic Psyrri (immediately north of Thissio), crumbling, graffiti-slathered buildings coexist with hip nightclubs, touristy tavernas with live traditional music, and highly conceptual café/bars. Gazi—the center of Athens' gay community—feels more local and authentically lively—but young. You'll find clubs, bars, and restaurants on the streets spiraling out from its main square (which, conveniently, surrounds the Keramikos Metro stop).

Outdoor Cinema: Screenings, which take place most nights in summer, come with folding chairs and small tables for your drinks (roughly June-Sept, sometimes in May and Oct). Try one of these venues: Aigli Village Cinema (at the Zappeion in the National Garden, tel. 210-336-9369, www.aeglizappiou.gr), Cine Paris (in the Plaka, overlooking Filomousou Square on the roof of Kidathineon 22, tel. 210-322-2071, www.cineparis.gr), and Cine Theseion (in Thissio at Apostolou Pavlou 7, tel. 210-347-0980, www.cine-thisio.gr).

Rooftop Bars: A touristy-yet-appealing way to spend an evening is at one of Athens' many rooftop bars, all with views of floodlit monuments. Try the A for Athens hotel or 360 Cocktail Bar (both on Monastiraki Square), the rooftop restaurant and bar of the Grande Bretagne Hotel (across the street from Syntagma Square), or the Thissio View restaurant and bar (Apostolou Pavlou 25).

Folk Dancing: The Dora Stratou Theater hosts Greece's best folk-dance company (late May-late Sept, daily except Mon and Tue, on southern side of Filopappos Hill, tel. 210-324-4395, after 19:30 call 210-921-4650, www.grdance.org).

Festivals: Athens' biggest party is the Athens & Epidavros Festival, highlighted by performances at the Odeon of Herodes Atticus. Tickets for the June-July festival generally go on sale three weeks in advance; same-day tickets are also sold at the theater box office (Mon-Fri 9:00-17:00, Sat 9:00-15:00, closed Sun, in the arcade at Panepistimiou 39, opposite the National Library, tel. 210-327-2000, www.greekfestival.gr).

Tours

Bus Tours: The well-regarded Hop In (tel. 210-428-5500, www.hopin.com), CHAT Tours (tel. 210-323-0827, www.chatours.gr), Key Tours (tel. 210-923-3166, www.keytours.gr), and GO Tours (tel. 210-921-9555, www.gotours.com.gr) offer tours within and outside of Athens. Various options are a bus-plus-walking tour of Athens (with guided Acropolis visit); a night city tour that finishes with dinner and folk dancing at a taverna; and day-long tours to Delphi and to Mycenae, Nafplio, and Epidavros.

Hop-On, Hop-Off Bus Tours: For a city overview and an easy way to reach outlying sights, consider hop-on, hop-off buses from CitySightseeing Athens (€18, tel. 210-922-0604, www.citysightseeing.gr) or Athens Open Tour (€17, tel. 210-881-5207, www.athensopentour.com). The main stop is on Syntagma Square, though you can hop on and buy your ticket at any stop—look for signs around town.

Tourist Trains: Two trains do a sightseeing circuit through Athens' tourist zone. Catch the Sunshine Express on Aiolou street along the Hadrian's Library fence at Agora Square or near the entrance to the Acropolis Museum (€5, departs hourly 9:30-22:00, Oct-April Sat-Sun only, 50-minute loop, tel. 211-405-5373, www.athensbytrain.gr). The Athens Happy Train stops at the bottom of Syntagma Square or at Monastiraki Square (€6, 2/hour 9:00-24:00, 1-hour loop, hop-on, hop-off privileges at strategic stops, tel. 213-039-0888, www.athenshappytrain.com).

Walking Tours: Athens Walking Tours offers several walks, including an Acropolis and City Tour (€38 plus entry fees, daily at 9:30, 3 hours) and their combo Acropolis, City Tour, and Acropolis Museum Tour (€54 plus entry fees, daily at 9:30, 5.5 hours, tel. 210-884-7269, mobile 694-585-9662, www.athenswalkingtours.gr, Despina).

Local Guide: Effie Perperi is a fine private guide (€50/hour, mobile 697-739-6659, effieperperi@gmail.com).

RESOURCES FROM RICK STEVES

This Pocket guide is one of many books in my series on European travel, including *Rick Steves Greece: Athens & the Peloponnese*. I also produce a public television series, *Rick Steves' Europe,* and a public radio show, *Travel with Rick Steves.*

My mobile-friendly website, www.ricksteves.com, offers thousands of fun articles, videos, photos, and radio interviews organized by country; a wealth of money-saving tips for planning your dream trip; monthly travel news dispatches; my travel talks and travel blog; my latest guidebook updates (www.ricksteves.com/update); my free Rick Steves Audio Europe app, an online travel store, and information on European rail passes and our tours of Europe.

How was your trip? If you'd like to share your tips, concerns, and discoveries, please fill out the survey at www.ricksteves.com/feedback. It helps us and fellow travelers.

Greek Survival Phrases

Knowing a few phrases of Greek can help if you're traveling off the beaten path. Just learning the pleasantries (such as please and thank you) will improve your connections with locals, even in the bigger cities.

Because Greek words can be transliterated differently in English, I've also included the Greek spellings. Note that in Greek, a semicolon is used the same way we use a question mark.

Hello. (formal)	**Gia sas.**	Γειά σας.	yah sahs
Hi. / Bye. (informal)	**Gia.**	Γειά.	yah
Good morning.	**Kali mera.**	Καλή μέρα.	kah-**lee** meh-rah
Good afternoon.	**Kali spera.**	Καλή σπέρα.	kah-**lee** speh-rah
Do you speak English?	**Milate anglika?**	Μιλάτε αγγλικά;	mee-**lah**-teh ahn-glee-**kah**
Yes. / No.	**Ne. / Ohi.**	Ναι. / Όχι.	neh / **oh**-hee
I understand.	**Katalaveno.**	Καταλαβαίνω.	kah-tah-lah-**veh**-noh
I don't understand.	**Den katalaveno.**	Δεν καταλαβαίνω.	dehn kah-tah-lah-**veh**-noh
Please. (Also: You're welcome.)	**Parakalo.**	Παρακαλώ.	pah-rah-kah-**loh**
Thank you (very much).	**Efharisto (poli).**	Ευχαριστώ (πολύ).	ehf-hah-ree-**stoh** (poh-**lee**)
Excuse me. (Also: I'm sorry.)	**Sygnomi.**	Συγνώμη.	seeg-**noh**-mee
(No) problem.	**(Kanena) problima.**	(Κανένα) πρόβλημα	(kah-**neh**-nah) **prohv**-lee-mah
Good.	**Orea.**	Ωραία.	oh-**reh**-ah
Goodbye.	**Antio.**	Αντίο.	ahd-**yoh** (think "adieu")
Good night.	**Kali nikta.**	Καλή νύχτα.	kah-**lee** neek-tah
one / two	**ena / dio**	ένα / δύο	**eh**-nah / **dee**-oh
three / four	**tria / tessera**	τρία /τέσσερα	**tree**-ah / **teh**-seh-rah
five / six	**pente / exi**	πέντε / έξι	**peh**-deh / **ehk**-se
seven / eight	**efta / ohto**	εφτά / οχτώ	ehf-**tah** / oh-**toh**
nine / ten	**ennia / deka**	εννιά / δέκα	ehn-**yah** / **deh**-kah
hundred / thousand	**ekato / hilia**	εκατό / χίλια	eh-kah-**toh** / **heel**-yah
How much?	**Poso kani?**	Πόσο κάνει;	poh-soh **kah**-nee
euro	**evro**	ευρώ	ev-**roh**
Write it?	**Grapsete to?**	Γράψετε το;	**grahp**-seh-teh toh
Is it free?	**Ine dorean?**	Είναι δωρεάν;	**ee**-neh doh-ree-**ahn**
Is it included?	**Perilamvanete?**	Περιλαμβάνεται;	peh-ree-lahm-**vah**-neh-teh
Where can I find / buy...?	**Pou boro na vro / agoraso...?**	Που μπορώ να βρω / αγοράσω...;	poo boh-**roh** nah vroh / ah-goh-**rah**-soh
I'd like / We'd like...	**Tha ithela / Tha thelame...**	Θα ήθελα / Θα θέλαμε...	thah **ee**-theh-lah / thah **thehl**-lah-meh
...a room.	**...ena dhomatio.**	...ένα δωμάτιο.	**eh**-nah doh-**mah**-tee-oh

...a ticket to ___.	...ena isitirio gia ___.	...ένα εισιτήριο για ___.	**eh**-nah ee-see-**tee**-ree-oh yah ___
Is it possible?	Ginete?	Γίνεται;	**yee**-neh-teh
Where is...?	Pou ine...?	Που είναι...;	poo **ee**-neh
...the bus station	...o stathmos ton leoforion	...ο σταθμός των λεωφορίων	oh **stahth**-mohs tohn leh-oh-foh-**ree**-ohn
...the train station	...o stathmos tou trenou	...ο σταθμός του τρένου	oh **stahth**-mohs too **treh**-noo
...the tourist information office	...to grafeio enimerosis touriston	...το γραφείο ενημέρωσης τουριστών	too grah-**fee**-oh eh-nee-**meh**-roh-sis too-roh-**stohn**
...the toilet	...toualeta	...τουαλέτα	twah-**leh**-tah
men	andres	άντρες	**ahn**-drehs
women	gynekes	γυναικές	yee-**neh**-kehs
left / right	dexia / aristera	δεξιά / αριστερά	dehk-see-**ah** / ah-ree-steh-**rah**
straight	efthia	ευθεία	ehf-**thee**-ah
At what time...	Ti ora...	Τι ώρα...	tee **oh**-rah
...does this open / close?	...anigete / klinete?	...ανοίγετε / κλείνετε;	ah-**nee**-yeh-teh / **klee**-neh-teh
Just a moment.	Ena lepto.	Ένα λεπτό.	**eh**-nah lep-**toh**
now / soon / later	tora / se ligo / argotera	τώρα / σε λίγο / αργότερα	**toh**-rah / seh **lee**-goh / ar-**goh**-teh-rah
today / tomorrow	simera / avrio	σήμερα / αύριο	**see**-meh-rah / **ahv**-ree-oh

In the Restaurant

I'd like to reserve...	Tha ithela na kliso...	Θα ήθελα να κλείσω...	thah **ee**-theh-lah nah **klee**-soh
We'd like to reserve...	Tha thelame na klisoume...	Θα θέλαμε να κλείσουμε...	thah **theh**-lah-meh nah **klee**-soo-meh
...a table for one / two.	...ena trapezi gia enan / dio.	...ένα τραπέζι για έναν / δύο.	eh-nah trah-**peh**-zee yah **eh**-nahn / **dee**-oh
non-smoking	mi kapnizon	μη καπνίζων	mee kahp-**nee**-zohn
Is this table free?	Ine eleftero afto to trapezi?	Είναι ελεύθερο αυτό το τραπέζι;	**ee**-neh eh-**lef**-teh-roh ahf-**toh** toh trah-**peh**-zee
The menu (in English), please.	Ton katalogo (sta anglika) parakalo.	Τον κατάλογο (στα αγγλικά) παρακαλώ.	tohn kah-**tah**-loh-goh (stah ahn-glee-**kah**) pah-rah-kah-**loh**
service (not) included	to servis (den) perilamvanete	το σέρβις (δεν) περιλαμβάνεται	toh **sehr**-vees (dehn) peh-ree-lahm-**vah**-neh-teh
cover charge	kouver	κουβέρ	koo-**vehr**
"to go"	gia exo	για έξω	yah **ehk**-soh
with / without	me / horis	με / χωρίς	meh / hoh-**rees**
and / or	ke / i	και / ή	keh / ee
fixed-price meal	menu	μενού	meh-**noo**

specialty of the house	i specialite tou magaziou	η σπεσιαλιτέ του μαγαζιού	ee speh-see-ah-lee-teh too mah-gah-zee-oo
half-portion	misi merida	μισή μερίδα	mee-see meh-ree-dah
daily special	to piato tis meras	το πιάτο της μέρας	toh pee-ah-toh tees meh-rahs
appetizers	proto piato	πρώτο πιάτο	proh-toh pee-ah-toh
bread	psomi	ψωμί	psoh-mee
cheese	tiri	τυρί	tee-ree
sandwich	sandwich or toast	σάντουιτς, τόστ	"sandwich," "toast"
soup	soupa	σούπα	soo-pah
salad	salata	σαλάτα	sah-lah-tah
meat	kreas	κρέας	kray-ahs
poultry / chicken	poulerika / kotopoulo	πουλερικά / κοτόπουλο	poo-leh-ree-kah / koh-toh-poo-loh
fish / seafood	psari / psarika	ψάρι / ψαρικά	psah-ree / psah-ree-kah
shellfish	thalassina	θαλασσινά	thah-lah-see-nah
fruit	frouta	φρούτα	froo-tah
vegetables	lahanika	λαχανικά	lah-hah-nee-kah
dessert	gliko	γλυκό	lee-koh
(tap) water	nero (tis vrisis)	νερό (της βρύσης)	neh-roh (tees vree-sees)
mineral water	metalliko nero	μεταλλικό νερό	meh-tah-lee-koh neh-roh
milk	gala	γάλα	gah-lah
(orange) juice	himos (portokali)	χυμός (πορτοκάλι)	hee-mohs (por-toh-kah-lee)
coffee	kafes	καφές	kah-fehs
tea	tsai	τσάι	chah-ee
wine (spoken)	krasi	κρασί	krah-see
wine (printed on label)	inos	οίνος	ee-nohs
red / white	kokkino / aspro	κόκκινο / άσπρο	koh-kee-noh / ah-sproh
sweet / dry / semi-dry	gliko / ksiro / imixiro	γλυκό / ξηρό / ημίξηρο	lee-koh / ksee-roh / ee-meek-see-roh
glass / bottle	potiri / boukali	ποτήρι / μπουκάλι	poh-tee-ree / boo-kah-lee
beer	bira	μπύρα	bee-rah
Here you are. (when given food)	Oriste.	Ορίστε.	oh-ree-steh
Enjoy your meal!	Kali orexi!	Καλή όρεξη!	kah-lee oh-rehk-see
(To your) health! (like "Cheers!")	(Stin i) gia mas!	(Στην υ) γειά μας!	(stee nee) yah mahs
Another.	Allo ena.	Άλλο ένα.	ah-loh eh-nah
Bill, please.	Ton logariasmo parakalo.	Τον λογαριασμό παρακαλώ.	tohn loh-gah-ree-ahs-moh pah-rah-kah-loh
tip	bourbouar	μπουρμπουάρ	boor-boo-ar
Very good!	Poli oreo!	Πολύ ωραίο!	poh-lee oh-ray-oh
Delicious!	Poli nostimo!	Πολύ νόστιμο!	poh-lee nohs-tee-moh

INDEX

Start your trip at

Our website enhances this book and turns

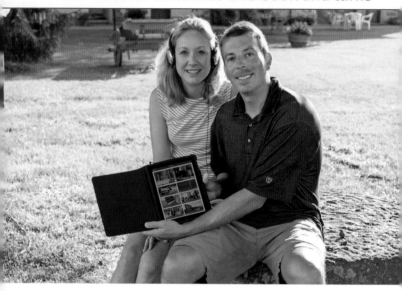

Explore Europe

At ricksteves.com you can browse through thousands of articles, videos, photos and radio interviews, plus find a wealth of money-saving travel tips for planning your dream trip. And with our mobile-friendly website, you can easily access all this great travel information anywhere you go.

TV Shows

Preview the places you'll visit by watching entire half-hour episodes of Rick Steves' Europe (choose from all 100 shows) on-demand, for free.

ricksteves.com

your travel dreams into affordable reality

Radio Interviews

Enjoy ready access to Rick's vast library of radio interviews covering

travel tips and cultural insights that relate specifically to your Europe travel plans.

Travel Forums

Learn, ask, share! Our online community of savvy travelers is a great resource for first-time travelers to Europe, as well as seasoned pros. You'll find forums on each country, plus travel tips and restaurant/hotel reviews. You can even ask one of our well-traveled staff to chime in with an opinion.

Travel News

Subscribe to our free Travel News e-newsletter, and get monthly updates from Rick on what's happening in Europe.

Audio Europe™

Rick's Free Travel App

Get your FREE Rick Steves Audio Europe™ app to enjoy...

- Dozens of self-guided tours of Europe's top museums, sights and historic walks

- Hundreds of tracks filled with cultural insights and sightseeing tips from Rick's radio interviews

- All organized into handy geographic playlists

- For Apple and Android

With Rick whispering in your ear, Europe gets even better.

Find out more at ricksteves.com

Pack Light and Right

Rick Steves has

Experience maximum Europe

Save time and energy

This guidebook is your
independent-travel toolkit. But
for all it delivers, it's still up to you
to devote the time and energy it
takes to manage the preparation
and logistics that are essential for a

happy trip. If that's a hassle, there's
a solution.

Rick Steves Tours

A Rick Steves tour takes you to
Europe's most interesting places
with great guides and small groups

great tours, too!

with minimum stress

of 28 or less. We follow Rick's favorite itineraries, ride in comfy buses, stay in family-run hotels, and bring you intimately close to the Europe you've traveled so far to see. Most importantly, we take away the logistical headaches so you can focus on the fun.

Join the fun

This year we'll take thousands of free-spirited travelers—nearly half of them repeat customers—along with us on four dozen different itineraries, from Ireland to Italy to Istanbul. Is a Rick Steves tour the right fit for your travel dreams? Find out at ricksteves.com, where you can also request Rick's latest tour catalog.

Europe is best experienced with happy travel partners. We hope you can join us.

See our itineraries at ricksteves.com

Rick Steves®

Nearly all Rick Steves guides are available as ebooks. Check with your favorite bookseller.

Rick Steves guidebooks are published by Avalon Travel, an imprint of Perseus Books, a Hachette Book Group company.

Maximize your travel skills with a good guidebook.

Milan & the Italian Lakes District
Naples & the Amalfi Coast
Northern Ireland
Norway
Sevilla, Granada & Southern Spain
St. Petersburg, Helsinki & Tallinn
Stockholm

POCKET GUIDES

Amsterdam
Athens
Barcelona
Florence
Italy's Cinque Terre
London
Munich & Salzburg
Paris
Prague
Rome
Venice
Vienna

TRAVEL CULTURE

Europe 101
European Christmas
Postcards from Europe
Travel as a Political Act

RICK STEVES' EUROPE DVDs

12 New Shows 2015–2016
Austria & the Alps
The Complete Collection 2000-2016

Eastern Europe
England & Wales
European Christmas
European Travel Skills & Specials
France
Germany, BeNeLux & More
Greece, Turkey & Portugal
The Holy Land: Israelis & Palestinians Today
Iran
Ireland & Scotland
Italy's Cities
Italy's Countryside
Scandinavia
Spain
Travel Extras

PHRASE BOOKS & DICTIONARIES

French
French, Italian & German
German
Italian
Portuguese
Spanish

PLANNING MAPS

Britain, Ireland & London
Europe
France & Paris
Germany, Austria & Switzerland
Ireland
Italy
Spain & Portugal

RickSteves.com 🇫 🇹 **@RickSteves**

Rick Steves books are available at bookstores
and through online booksellers.

PHOTO CREDITS

Title Page
© Rick Steves
Table of Contents
© Carol Ries
Introduction
© Laura VanDeventer, Rick Steves, Carol Ries
Athens City Walk
© Aaron Harting, Rick Steves, Gretchen Strauch, Cameron Hewitt, Gene Openshaw, Lauren Mills, Carol Ries, Laura VanDeventer
Acropolis
page 49, Temple of Nike © Greek photonews/Alamy
All other photos © Cameron Hewitt, Rick Steves, Gene Openshaw, Sandra Hundacker, Gretchen Strauch, Laura VanDeventer, Bruce VanDeventer, Wikimedia Commons (PD-Art/PD-US)
Ancient Agora
© Gene Openshaw, Rick Steves, Carol Ries, Cameron Hewitt, Laura VanDeventer, David Willet
Acropolis Museum
page 91, Hekatompedon © PRISMA ARCHIVO/Alamy
page 93, Pensive Athena Relief © Ancient Art & Architecture Collection Ltd/Alamy; Nike Adjusting Her Sandal Relief © The Art Gallery Collection/Alamy
page 97, The Parthenon Frieze © Peter Horree/Alamy
All other photos © Rick Steves, Cameron Hewitt
National Archaeological Museum
© Cameron Hewitt, Rick Steves, Gene Openshaw
Athens Sights
© Laura VanDeventer, Cameron Hewitt, Rick Steves, Sandra Hundacker, Cathy Lu
Sleeping
page 139 © Art Gallery Hotel
Eating
© Carol Ries, Rick Steves
Practicalities
© Rick Steves

Avalon Travel
An imprint of Perseus Books
A Hachette Book Group company
1700 Fourth Street
Berkeley, CA 94710, USA

Printed in China by RR Donnelley
Second Edition.
First printing May 2017.

ISBN 978-1-63121-557-5
ISSN 2165-0802

For the latest on Rick's lectures, books, tours, public-radio show, and public-television
series, contact Rick Steves' Europe, 130 Fourth Avenue North, Edmonds, WA 98020, tel.
425/771-8303, www.ricksteves.com, rick@ricksteves.com.

RICK STEVES' EUROPE
Managing Editor: Jennifer Madison Davis
Special Publications Manager: Risa Laib
Editors: Glenn Eriksen, Tom Griffin, Katherine Gustafson, Suzanne Kotz, Cathy Lu,
Carrie Shepherd
Editorial & Production Assistant: Jessica Shaw
Editorial Interns: Grace Swanson, Chelsea Wing
Researcher: Cathy Lu
Graphic Content Director: Sandra Hundacker
Maps & Graphics: David C. Hoerlein, Lauren Mills, Mary Rostad

AVALON TRAVEL
Senior Editor and Series Manager: Madhu Prasher
Editor: Jamie Andrade
Associate Editor: Sierra Machado
Copy Editor: Kelly Lydick
Proofreader: Becca Freed
Indexer: Stephen Callahan
Production & Typesetting: McGuire Barber Design
Cover Design: Kimberly Glyder Design
Interior Design: Darren Alessi
Maps & Graphics: Kat Bennett, Mike Morgenfeld
Front Cover Image: © Freesurf69 | Dreamstime.com

ABOUT THE AUTHORS

Rick Steves

Since 1973, Rick has spent about four months a year exploring Europe. His mission: to empower Americans to have European trips that are fun, affordable, and culturally broadening. Rick produces a best-selling guidebook series, a public television series, and a public radio show, and organizes small-group tours that take over 20,000 travelers to Europe annually. He does all of this with the help of a hardworking, well-traveled staff of 100 at Rick Steves' Europe in Edmonds, Washington, near Seattle. When not on the road, Rick is active in his church and with advocacy groups focused on economic justice, drug policy reform, and ending hunger. To recharge, Rick plays piano, relaxes at his family cabin in the Cascade Mountains, and spends time with his partner Trish, son Andy, and daughter Jackie. Find out more about Rick at www.ricksteves.com and on Facebook.

Gene Openshaw

Gene has co-authored a dozen *Rick Steves* books, specializing in writing walks and tours of Europe's cities, museums, and cultural sights. He also contributes to Rick's public television series, produces tours for Rick Steves Audio Europe, and is a regular guest on Rick's public radio show. Outside of the travel world, Gene has co-authored *The Seattle Joke Book*. As a composer, Gene has written a full-length opera called *Matter* (soundtrack available on Amazon), a violin sonata, and dozens of songs. He lives near Seattle with his daughter, enjoys giving presentations on art and history, and roots for the Mariners in good times and bad.

Cameron Hewitt

Born in Denver and raised in central Ohio, Cameron settled in Seattle in 2000. Ever since, he has spent three months each year in Europe, contributing to guidebooks, tours, radio and television shows, and other media for Rick Steves' Europe, where he serves as content manager. Cameron married his high school sweetheart (and favorite travel partner), Shawna, and enjoys taking pictures, trying new restaurants, and planning his next trip.

FOLDOUT COLOR MAP ▶

The foldout map on the opposite page includes:

- **Maps of Athens on one side**
- **Maps of Greece, Athens transit, and the port of Piraeus on the other side**